P9-BID-165

108 ANSWERS

Asking About Zen

108 ANSWERS

Asking About Zen

JIHO SARGENT

WITHDRAWN

New York · WEATHERHILL · *Tokyo*

Illustrations by Tadashi Hirota.

First edition, 2001
Copyright © 2001 by A. W. Sargent
Published by Weatherhill, Inc.
41 Monroe Turnpike, Trumbull, Connecticut 06611

Protected by copyright under the terms of the International Copyright Union; all rights reserved. Except for fair use in book reviews, no part of this book may be reproduced by any means, including any method of photographic reproduction, without permission of the publisher.

Printed in the United States.

Library of Congress Cataloging-in-Publication Data available upon request.

CONTENTS

SHATFORD LIBRARY

OCT   2008

1570 E. Colorado Blvd.
Pasadena, CA 91106

ZEN IN THEORY

WITHDRAWN

ZAZEN IN PRACTICE

WHAT IS A ZEN PRIEST?

WHAT ARE ZEN RELIGIOUS SERVICES LIKE?

WHAT TITLES AND HONORIFICS
ARE USED FOR ZEN PRIESTS?

WHAT CHARACTERIZES JAPANESE BUDDHISM
OVERALL AND ZEN BUDDHISM IN PARTICULAR?

ABOUT MYSELF

ASKING ABOUT ZEN

108 Answers

ZEN IN THEORY

1. Why Zen?

In a world full of religious movements, why is it that Zen Buddhism has caught and held so much attention in the West, far from its Asian homelands, for the last fifty years? Why is it that people around the world have followed the plethora of movements mushrooming under the name of Zen and its characteristic practice of the motionless, seated contemplation called *zazen*? How do the Western-based movements relate to the religious teachings that have been practiced in Asia for two and a half millennia? These are questions that allow no simple answers. All we can do is to consider a few of the factors that have been observed to influence Western people who have come to Zen as a new religion—or as an exercise for mental or physical health, as an adjunct to martial arts or Eastern healing practices, as a method of dealing with pain, or simply as something that has aroused their curiosity.

People come to an active participation in religion for many reasons, most of which reflect some sort of difficulty in their lives. Zen Buddhism is no different from any other religion in that sense. Those who remain active participants are those who discover a value in participation.

For Zen, that value resides in the direct experience of religious truth that can occur in zazen and the consequent change in attitudes and actions toward greater harmony and less conflict. Even the first experience of zazen often makes a deep impression because of the stillness and silence. For most of us, it is the first time in our lives when we have simply sat still, not moving, not speaking, and not reacting to our environment. For most of us, it is the first time in our lives when we have given ourselves an opportunity to perceive ourselves and our environment in their reality, without the layers of filtering imposed by habitual concepts and judgments. A glimpse of unmasked reality, no matter how momentary, can forever change our ways of viewing, and of living, our lives. That direct view, so difficult to achieve, is what Buddhism calls opening one's eyes, or awakening.

Other branches of Buddhism, as well as other religions, can lead to the same perceptions, but it is overwhelmingly Zen that has attracted and maintained the participation of Westerners from all walks of life. During the second half of the twentieth century, Zen Buddhism suddenly expanded from a small, conservative branch of Japan's established religions to a household word around the world. As people sought a new religion, something free of the constrictions they felt in their mainstream, established religions, why did the search so often lead to the quintessentially formal, disciplined practice of zazen?

I think the answer lies in a number of factors, some historical, some fundamental to all Buddhism, some peculiar to Zen Buddhism, and some arising from Western misconceptions concerning Asian cultures and religions. Zen's "brand recognition" is a product of history. Its freedom of belief results from the most basic of all Buddhist teachings. That it is often viewed as something apart from religion is an effect of interactions between the Buddhist understanding of what constitutes religion and the prevailing Western view of the same question. Misunderstandings, quite naturally, abound. Along with the misunderstandings of the nature of Buddhist religion come the faulty ideas that Zen means freedom from rituals and from the need for studying difficult ancient texts. Zen offers a religion that accepts science. And in startling leaps of thought that seem based primarily on faulty translations by early Western scholars of Buddhism, Zen is thought to offer a monasticism without a monastic rule and to produce certified mystic experiences. Regrettably, the mistranslations have taken on a life of their own and are even more entrenched today than in the time of their origination.

Let's briefly examine each of these factors, starting with what is probably the most common and most attractive.

The most compelling reason for Westerners starting and continuing Zen practice has surely been the promise of mystical experience. Not only a moment of mystic insight that can be treasured within oneself, but the confirmation of that insight by someone who has previously been confirmed as having experienced a similar insight. And this leads normally to some form of public recognition of the insight. What more could an apprentice mystic desire!

Mystic experience is one of the "yes and no" points of Buddhism. Yes, it most certainly occurs. No, no one can guarantee that such an experience will occur to you. Yes, when it occurs the experience is profoundly affecting. But no, it is far from ensuring that one's future actions will approach a Buddhist ideal or even avoid acts that are condemned everywhere.

The experience is, like any experience of reality in our human lives, the matter of a single instant and vanishes before we know it has come. Clinging to that instant is a form of desire, which Buddhism wisely recommends that we avoid.

Yes, some—probably not all—persons who have experienced a profound insight are able to evaluate whether another person's experience is of a similar order. No, this does not really mean anything to either evaluator or the one evaluated. What matters is how each person's way of living proceeds.

It certainly is to be hoped that all members of the clergy of a religion, Zen Buddhism or any other, have a thorough comprehension of the primary teachings of the religion. In the case of Buddhism, this is termed having opened one's eyes or being awakened. The awakening may come about in many ways, certainly including zazen or koan practice, but just as certainly not limited to those practices. I have frequently heard Westerners express the notion that all Zen clerics must, or at least should, have had a deep mystic experience. I do not recall ever hearing a Japanese express such a thought. Once I estimated the number of clerics who must complete their training each year just to maintain the present number of Zen temples. To do that, more than six hundred Japanese men and women would have to experience great mystical awakening every year, preferably before the age of thirty or so. Perhaps you are comfortable with that number as a reasonable expectation. I am not. What is asked of Zen clerics is that they care for their temple members, provide guidance and support to the community at large as well as their own temple's member families, and ensure that their temples will endure at least until the next generation is prepared to take over. It is not required that they be mystics or experience "altered states of consciousness."

If all this is true for the Zen clergy, how much more so for Zen lay-people. Whether Asians or Occidentals, Buddhists properly devote their full energies and attention to living this life in a way that increases the total compassion of the universe and decreases the total evil.

WIDELY RECOGNIZED NAME

The first reason for a widespread interest in Zen Buddhism is quite simply that the name is well known in the West. It is revealing, I think, that when Chinese, Vietnamese, and Korean Buddhist priests began establishing activities in the West, they used the Japanese term *Zen* in most cases rather than the Chinese, Vietnamese, or Korean name for the same set of teachings.

The beginnings of Zen in the United States occurred as early as the 1893 World Parliament of Religions, held as part of Chicago's Columbian Exposition. Among the participants was the distinguished Rinzai Zen priest Soyen Shaku. As a result of that participation, his lay follower D. T. Suzuki went to Chicago in 1897 to work with a publisher on English translations of Buddhist texts. The extensive works published by Dr. Suzuki from that time onward have constituted an introduction to Zen Buddhism for millions of Western readers.

It was after World War II ended, in 1945, that Zen truly began to grow in the United States, then in all of North America, South America, and Western Europe. Later it extended into Eastern Europe, Oceania, and as far as Africa. By the late 1960s, Americans of all types had heard the name Zen as a mystical Japanese religion. Many even believed (and many still do) that all religion in Japan is Zen.

For those considering a change to a different religion, Zen's familiar name adds the security of long-established teachings to the stimulus of teachings far removed from the monotheistic beliefs constituting the Western religious mainstream.

FREEDOM OF BELIEF

Zen Buddhism, like all Buddhism, has nothing to say on the topic of gods, either singular or plural. An early Buddhist scripture says that Shakyamuni Buddha (the Awakened One of the Shakya people) once was asked whether gods exist. He replied that the answer to that question has no bearing on our conduct in this life, so we should not waste valuable time in considering it.

Anyone can thus begin, and long continue, the practice of zazen and the study of Buddhism without any need to accept a new god or discard a previously accepted one. Indeed, Zen in the West is often completely divorced from its Buddhist context. And it is often stated that Buddhism itself is not a religion because it has no god.

This basic fact of Buddhist thought makes it relatively easy, I think, for Westerners to enter Zen from a background of monotheistic religion.

CAN BE CONSIDERED SOMETHING APART FROM RELIGION

It seems often to be the case that Westerners who have rejected established Western religions come to Zen, specifically to the practice of zazen, as something completely unrelated to religion. Zen does not ask one to believe; it suggests that one act (or, in zazen, refrain from action).

The idea that Buddhism is not a religion makes it possible for even clerics of other religions to participate in zazen and other Buddhist practices. Especially in Europe, zazen has become very popular among Roman Catholic monastics.

Several groups in the United States have divorced their Zen from Buddhism and use zazen as a method of psychotherapy or personal growth.

This approach has circled back to Japan, with some groups rejecting any connection with the established sects of traditional Zen Buddhism, concentrating solely on the practice of zazen, and creating instructors in place of clerics. The instructors do not perform the various religious observances that are important to Japan's Buddhism; instead they devote themselves solely to the promotion of zazen and its related koan practice.

One of the main problems with this outlook is that it promotes a disregard for the Buddhist teachings concerning the meaning of opening one's eyes and describing the way of life that naturally results from a thoroughgoing comprehension of the realities of the universe.

FREEDOM FROM RITUALS

Although Zen Buddhism, as one of Japan's established religions, includes many ritual observances, even within Japan the laypeople who participate in zazen practice seldom are those who attend the temple's other observances.

The funeral and later memorial services for a family member, for example, are likely to be held in a temple other than that where zazen is done. (Most people remain members of their traditional family temple regardless of its sect. If they become interested in some special practice such as zazen, or the teachings of another sect, or the explanations of a particular priest, they feel no need to change their temple membership to suit that interest.)

Few of the Western Zen centers perform any of the Zen observances maintained in Japan. The center leader, whether holding the status of a priest or remaining a layperson, often has no training in the conduct and meaning of those observances. Westerners averse to the rites of the monotheistic religions they are familiar with tend to view this separation of ritual practices from zazen (which, remember, they often view as a practice apart from religion) as an ideal situation.

DIFFICULT ANCIENT TEXTS NEED NOT BE MASTERED

Most of Buddhism, and of other widespread Eastern religions, requires the reading of texts in languages and writing systems that are very little known in the West. Zen instead speaks of "a special transmission outside of the scriptures." That phrase, shorn of its many layers of connotation, is perhaps the best-known Zen saying in the West.

In fact, Zen Buddhism has generated a huge literature of its own and maintained the use and study of the shared Buddhist scriptures. Collections of koans allude extensively to the entire range of antecedent Buddhist texts (not to mention the allusions to classical Chinese literature).

At least at the beginning, however, Zen practitioners can easily avoid language study. Most Western Zen groups use English translations or transliterations of sutras (Buddhist scriptures) if, indeed, they chant sutras at all. In recent years, English translations of Buddhist texts in general, and Zen texts in particular, have been a growth industry, particularly in academia. The inquiring mind that lacks knowledge of Asian languages thus has a range of resources.

RELIGION THAT AGREES WITH SCIENCE

Another advantage of Buddhism in relation to Western minds is its acceptance of modern science. This is true of all varieties of Buddhism, but has perhaps been noted most often with regard to the Zen branch.

Buddhism does have a traditional cosmology, but it does not ask anyone to take that ancient cosmology as a literal truth. Many of the oldest Buddhist concepts seem to prefigure modern scientific concepts. So a person coming to Buddhism has no need to deny the whole body of today's science or any part of it.

"MONASTICISM" WITHOUT RULES

The institution of monasticism, with monks and nuns consecrating their lives to religious devotion, doubtless became romanticized in the popular mind almost at the moment of its inception. Accidents of history acted in concert with the human fondness for viewing the new in terms of the familiar to establish a Western impression that Buddhism (and Buddhism alone) is a wholly monastic religion. Not for Buddhism, goes this line of thought, the unfortunate Catholic dichotomy of monastics sheltered behind walls versus secular priests dealing with laypeople; all Buddhist clerics without exception are viewed as monastics. That this would leave no one at all to tend to the religious concerns of ordinary adherents is a detail that has been readily overlooked in the West.

The observable fact that Japan's Buddhist clergy has no requirement, or even admiration, for such rules as poverty, chastity, and obedience seems to have been accepted without in any way discouraging the monastic thesis. The fact that Japan's Buddhist history consistently shows a general pattern of one or two clerics per residence has been simply ignored. The inclusion of women in Japan's clergy has been made to reinforce the monastic thesis, inasmuch as Christian rules gave women no clerical role until recent decades and still, in Catholicism, forbid the entry of women into the clergy. Because many Buddhist traditions have women performing religious rites, goes this misconception, all persons performing those rites must be lay monastics, be they male or female.

Be all that as it may, Westerners raised on the romance of monastic purity were delighted to discover a "Zen monasticism" that they could enjoy without the inconveniences of cloistered communal life, obedience to superiors, rejection of personal property, and abstention from sexual relations. Even married couples could participate in this new institution of monasticism. The only difficulty perceived was how to incorporate children into the monastery.

2. Why do people do zazen?

One noted Japanese priest, the Reverend Suigan Yogo, often said that we do zazen simply because we hear the sound of the zazen bell. Those who do not do zazen, he said, have not yet heard the bell.

Most of our daily actions are purposeful actions: we perform an action to obtain a desired result. That is the way our minds usually operate. To some extent, it probably is a way of thinking that we cannot entirely avoid. In principle, though, zazen should be practiced only because the practice of zazen is a natural part of our lives.

Of course we all have reasons for starting zazen. If we did not, our ears would never open to the sound of the bell. What makes the difference is how we handle those reasons once we have established a normal place in our lives for zazen.

One common reason for an interest in zazen is a wish for a calmer, quieter mind. This always reminds me of a time when I was late going to an evening zazen meeting after work. The route from my apartment included a steep hill just before the temple. So I entered the hall for zazen still gasping a bit from hurrying up the hill. The starting three bells sounded as I tried to quiet both breathing and thinking, which was spinning resentfully on the task that had kept me working late and the train schedule that meant I had to wait for two trains on my way home. Naturally the more I tried to clamp a calm over my agitation, the more agitated I felt. It was only when I was able to let go of the time preceding the moment in which I was living that my breathing and thoughts returned to their zazen quiet. The person who tries to obtain a quiet mind through zazen probably does feel calmer and quieter during the first several periods of zazen. It is rare for most of us to remain silent and motionless for even five minutes, let alone thirty to fifty minutes, so the experience of that state naturally conduces to calm. Sooner or later, though, there comes a circumstance similar to my run up the hill. Then the sitter perches on a cushion thinking, "I have a quiet mind, I Have A Quiet Mind, I HAVE A QUIET MIND!" with jaws not merely closed but clamped tight and muscles not simply motionless but rigid. And the next thought is, "This zazen is no use at all! I quit." Before trying to use zazen as a means to a quiet mind, you might well pause to consider where that mind is going to come from. Will you just snatch it from the air as you perch on your cushion? You can only have a quiet mind after zazen if you had a quiet mind before it. The most that zazen can do is to provide an opportunity for your quiet mind to evidence itself.

Another reason given for starting zazen is a need to deal with pain. Although it is true that zazen techniques can help in this area, concentration on pain relief is likely to preclude any religious involvement.

The idea popularized by the Beat Zen movement, still popular among both young people and those not so young, is that zazen leads to a different (presumably higher) level of consciousness or mystical experience. Many of the Americans who took up Zen in the 1960s were people who used drugs for that purpose. They viewed zazen as a way of achieving a drug experience without the need for drugs. I'm sure that doing something without drugs is healthier than doing it with drugs, but the whole pursuit is not only outside religion but actively inimical to religion. The search for such an experience is self-defeating, though it is true that the mind of total absorption in the universe of this instant is a different experience from our ordinary minds full of discursive thought and opinions. Striving for a particular experience necessitates some preconception about that experience. There are basically only two responses in such a situation. Either one manages to fabricate something resembling what has been said, or imagined, about the target experience, or one steadfastly refuses to accept anything that may even slightly relate to the experience that has been said or imagined. Remember the joke about "Don't think about a purple elephant"?

This leaves us with the most common reason for undertaking any sort of religious practice: a sense that life is not satisfactory in one way or another, to one degree or another. This can be triggered by something as trivial as a sequence of dark, rainy days or as tragic as the death of a child. The first of Shakyamuni Buddha's Four Noble Truths, usually phrased in English as "all life is suffering," should rather, based on the Indic phrasing, be "all human life is unsatisfying." At least so I have been told—I am no Sanskritist. The Buddhist response to that truth is the other three noble truths: The causes of unsatisfactoriness are birth, old age, illness, and death; there is an end to unsatisfactoriness; the way to that end is the Eightfold Path. Zen practice is one way of following the Eightfold Path that leads to the reality of human life and thus to fulfillment in this life.

We are not all modern-day Shakyamunis; most of us manage only occasional glimpses of reality that help us to live this life as it truly is. Even a brief experience of zazen can grant us a small experience of reality. A longer experience of zazen can provide the opportunity for a larger experience of reality. The person whose zazen is an attempt to achieve some preconceived goal is doomed to false joy or true disappointment. The person whose zazen is simply sitting and experiencing the whole reality of one moment will probably soon discover that life seems, in some indefinable way, to be smoother, less unsatisfying, despite the many ups and downs of passing phenomena.

3. What is "just sitting"?

The Sōtōshū practice of *shikan taza* is often translated as "just sitting." The "just" part of this phrase (the *shikan* part of the Japanese term) means that there is no part of the person that is not completely engaged in zazen.

In his *General Advice on the Principles of Zazen* (Fukanzazengi), Sōtōshū's founder Dōgen Zenji instructed us as follows:

> Let go of all associations, and put all affairs aside.
> Do not think of either good or evil.
> Do not be concerned with either right or wrong.
> Put aside the operation of your intellect, volition, and consciousness.
> Stop considering things with your memory, imagination, and contemplation.
> Do not seek to become Buddha.

and later,

> Think of not-thinking.
> How do you think of not-thinking?
> Beyond-thinking.
> That is the essential way of zazen.

The practice of just sitting is founded in Dōgen's inversion of the usual Buddhist formulation for awakening. Instead of the generally taught sequence of living by the Buddhist precepts so that one can practice concentration (zazen) so that one can reach awakening, Dōgen taught that all beings are inherently awakened and therefore will naturally practice zazen, which will result in a life that accords with the Buddhist precepts.

It has been widely noted in recent years that many contemporary Zen leaders, both priests and laypeople, live in ways that are greatly at odds with the Buddhist precepts, no matter whether we interpret those precepts strictly or liberally (a matter discussed later, in two questions concerning the precepts for Zen priests and those for Zen laypeople). This does not invalidate Dōgen's teaching. It merely demonstrates the difficulty of actualizing our awakening and practicing true zazen. The unfortunate fact that some people do not appear to succeed should not lead us to reject the pos-

Just sitting does not mean rejecting the study of koans, any more than it means rejecting the recitation, copying, and study of sutras; it simply means that during the time for zazen, one devotes mind and body to zazen. Koans may be studied at other times, as useful guides to a Buddhist life. Sutras may be studied, copied, and recited at other times, as useful guides and as traditional religious practices in their own right. We have wide evidence that leading Zen priests from the earliest times through today have supported many forms of Buddhist learning and practice. Zen, and specifically "just sitting," is not a path of rejection but rather the acceptance of one particular practice, zazen, as a key element that supports and is, in turn, supported by the practices involving study and actions.

The primary difficulties of just sitting, I think, are the temptation to set zazen apart as a special practice that has no relationship to our daily lives, and an inclination to involve ourselves in distractions instead of devoting the utmost energy to our zazen.

4. What is a koan?

First, what is it *not?* A koan is *not* a puzzle or riddle. Puzzles and riddles are solved through the very discursive thinking and logic that koans are meant to discourage.

Literally, *kō* means "public," and *an* means "record." The Chinese term, *kung-an,* originally designated a government decree or a legal case that had established a precedent. The Zen use of the term designates a brief text, usually a dialogue, that encapsulates a particular Buddhist teaching or characterizes the teachings of a particular priest. Koan practice began in China during the T'ang dynasty (618–907). The period during which both Rinzai and Sōtō teachings were transmitted to Japan, and when many Japanese priests studied in China, was near the end of the Sung dynasty (960–1126), which coincided with the peak in popularity of koans in China. There are said to be about 1,700 koans that were composed in China.

My own encounter with koans began when I helped with the English portion of a Sōtōshū temple's bulletin. Each issue contained an essay by one of the priests at that temple, and the priest writing the essays usually chose a koan as the topic. (Koans are popular as topics for essays and lectures, even in non-Zen sects of Buddhism.)

A problem occurred with a koan about a Chinese priest and one of his trainees. Simply stated, Baso (in Chinese, Ma-tsu Tao-i, 709–788) had been earnestly practicing zazen for more than ten years in a small hermitage on the temple grounds. One day the chief priest, Nangaku (in Chinese, Nan-yueh Huai-jang, 677–744) came to the hermitage and asked, "What have you been doing lately?" Baso answered that he had been doing nothing but zazen. When Nangaku asked why he did that, Baso replied, "To become a buddha." At that, Nangaku picked up a piece of tile lying nearby and began to polish it. Baso asked, "What are you doing?" Nangaku answered that he was polishing the tile. When Baso asked why he was doing that, Nangaku replied, "To make it into a mirror."

One indisputable point about this koan is that making a mirror from a piece of tile is meant to be an impossible task. But I thought about the deep blue, shiny roof tiles on many Japanese temples. Probably they would not make very good mirrors, but if polished clean they seemed likely to be reflective. Finally I asked the essay writer about that. He said, "Oh, is *that* what you think of when you hear the word 'tile'! No, this koan means something that had a surface more like a brick." As the saying goes, suddenly I had an awakening. At least concerning "tiles."

That koan was generally understood to support a particular form of koan practice developed shortly before Dōgen went to China, yet Dōgen chose to quote it in support of his own teaching that awakening is identical with zazen, being neither cause nor effect. As is often the case with koans, a number of different lessons may be drawn from this story.

The sources of the classical koans include Chinese histories of Zen lineages, which record awakening histories and notable teachings; collections of sayings by particular priests, usually gathered by those who trained under the priest; and recorded collections of sermons for laypeople and private lectures for priest-trainees. The best-known koan collections, the *Hekiganroku, Shōyōroku,* and *Mumonkan,* were composed and published during the period between 1026 and 1166, using cases selected from earlier sources and adding extensive commentary to the bare koan narratives.

5. What is koan practice?

Koans are studied and used in many ways, but what is called "koan practice," or, in Japanese, *kanna zen,* is a formal practice under the direct supervision of a priest who has completed the entire set of koans used by a particular sect. The details of this practice generally follow the system devised by Hakuin Ekaku Rōshi (1686–1769). The popularity of this system got off to a good start through the actions of Hakuin's nearly one hundred apprentices, who opened priests halls (*sōdō* in Japanese) and followed the method their master had taught them.

Two "grandchildren," apprentices of one of Hakuin's apprentices, formally established the two Hakuin Zen systems that are still used today. In these systems, the daily life of those in a priests hall (mostly priest-trainees) is a tightly regulated round of zazen, koan study, indoor and outdoor labor, religious begging, and sutra chanting. This practice is performed in spring and autumn for three months each. Trainees can return to their home temples during the winter and summer quarters. The koans studied are those of classic koan collections, such as the *Hekiganroku,* plus some that were devised by Hakuin and never published but transmitted only by word of mouth to a student. The best known of these oral koans is one called the sound of one hand clapping.

My own experience with koan practice lasted only one day and was, as I later learned, highly unusual. A newspaper announcement during my first summer in Japan led me to a weeklong *sesshin* "for foreign women," to be held in a temple of one of Rinzaishū's smaller sects. A small zazen hall provided the one-tatami-mat spaces on which we did zazen, slept, and ate the two formal meals each day. Attendees turned out to be a young English woman, a Japanese woman probably in her late twenties, and my forty-seven-year-old self. When Fiona and I were summoned to the priest's interview room, I discovered that I had been appointed "interpreter" for Fiona, whose Japanese was even more limited than mine, despite the fact that my language ability was grossly insufficient for my own understanding, let alone for interpreting for someone else. The priest's English had, we found, been largely exhausted with welcoming us and giving zazen instructions. Confusion thus reigned from the moment we entered the main building, where the interview room was located.

As coached, we rang a bell to request entrance, then waited for the summoning bell struck by the priest. We entered, bowed to the altar and to the priest, and sat side by side in our best approximation of *seiza,* the kneeling posture with buttocks on heels that is used on all formal occasions. The priest told us our koan was (to the best of my comprehension then and recollection now) "Sitting is the zazen of the body. What is the zazen of the mind?" We were instructed to hold that question in mind throughout all our activities and even while sleeping. Then we were dismissed by a bell tone and bowed ourselves out, returning to the zazen hall. At the first break time, Fiona and I discussed the question but had very little to offer each other, both being completely new to this experience. A day later, we once more went to the interview room. This time I was told to enter first and present my response. It was "shikan taza," a phrase prompted mostly by the fact that I knew its meaning in English. Then Fiona entered while I remained. Her response was *"mu,"* (literally "nothing" or "not"), probably on the same grounds as my own. Then the priest said (I think), "You are both wrong. You should have said, *satori.*" And that was the end of our koan practice.

Despite its brevity and idiosyncrasies, that experience incorporated the essential point of koan practice, striving to become one with the koan. Ruth Fuller Sasaki, among the first Westerners to become certified as a priest in Japan's Rinzaishū, described it this way:

> Proficiency in zazen is the basic ground for koan study. During the practice of zazen the koan is handled. To say that it is used as a subject of meditation is to state the fact incorrectly. The koan is taken over by the prepared instrument, and, when a fusion of instrument and device takes place, the state of consciousness is achieved which it is the intent of the koan to illumine and in this instant the koan is resolved. This experience may take place during formal zazen practice; it may as well be under any condition and at any time of the day or night.

In more traditional form, each student is initially assigned a koan by the instructor of the priests hall. Responses to the koan are presented once or twice a day except during sesshin, when they may be presented several times each day. This presentation of response, called *sanzen* (literally, participation in Zen), starts with a formal request and permission signaled by an exchange of bell tones, followed by bows to the floor. The student and instructor sit facing each other while the student states the assigned koan and gives a response. If the instructor accepts the response as valid for that koan, the student may be asked to choose a capping phrase for it, to be selected from a collection of Zen poems, for presentation next time. Otherwise the instructor rings the bell that signals the end of the interview, possibly first adding a word of encouragement or a hint toward the right direction.

The word satori is the noun form of *satoru,* a Japanese verb that means to open one's eyes, awaken, and see clearly. These words, especially the verb, are also used in everyday contexts and not exclusively as religious terms. Phrases offered as examples of the verb's use in one Japanese-English dictionary include "He will *know* better by and by," "He *took the hint* and left the place," and *"Realizing* the harmfulness of the vice, I have given up smoking."

Buddhism originated with the awakening of Shakyamuni Buddha when he sat motionless beneath a tree. In that awakening the Buddha clearly saw, as a part of his own being and sensations, what we now call the Four Noble Truths, the Eightfold Path, and the Twelve-Linked Chain of Dependent Origination.

This event in the life of the Buddha, as well as similar events in the lives of later Buddhists, is often spoken of in English as enlightenment. We must, I think, carefully consider the differing implications of the words enlightenment and awakening. Most importantly, awakening is something both performed and experienced by oneself. Although the time of awakening may be triggered by something external (in the ordinary way of thinking), the action is something entirely internal and solitary (again, in the ordinary way of thinking). Enlightenment, in contrast, is something that occurs only as a result of some action outside oneself. Whether in Buddhist speech or ordinary talk, we say "I was enlightened," or "She enlightened me." We never say "I enlightened" in the way that we often say "I awakened."

In the case of Shakyamuni Buddha and in the cases of all those who later experienced true satori, the experience of awakening, although it occurred in an instant, changed all the remainder of that person's life. Even though many years may pass before the full results of opening one's eyes become apparent to others, the one who awakens will see the universe differently from the very instant of awakening. The instant in itself is only an instant like any other; the results, which endure not only throughout the remaining life of the awakener but also throughout all that may be affected by that awakener, are a unique treasure.

When Zen first became popular in the West, those who took it up often falsely described satori as some kind of surrealistic rapture. They even stated that satori could be experienced through taking drugs.

Nothing could be more wrong than such notions. We may judge the experience of satori itself, I think, by considering the actions of Shakyamuni Buddha in the time immediately following his awakening.

Among the first Buddhist teachings recorded are several consistent stories of the period when Siddhartha Gautama, a young man who had spent years as a wandering religious seeker and ascetic, became the Awakened One (this is the literal meaning of the Indic term *buddha*). First, for seven days he remained motionless beneath a tree in contemplation of the full meaning of awakened truth. After that came further exploration of his new understanding while he sat beneath a series of other trees for seven days each. The number of weeks occupied by this contemplation is usually given as seven, although some versions list different numbers of trees and thus of weeks. Toward the end of this period, the Buddha turned his attention to the question of whether he could assist others in the path toward opening their eyes. At last he decided he must at least seek out the five men with whom he had practiced asceticism and try to convey to those five something of the truth to which he had awakened, hoping that in this way the five might also become able to open their eyes. This, then, was the first fruit of satori.

7. What is kenshō?

Kenshō is the special term applied sometimes to the first experience of Buddhist awakening and sometimes to any such awakening of ordinary persons, so that satori can be reserved to designate the awakening of the Buddha and of a small number of notable ancient Buddhists. The two Chinese characters used to write kenshō are, respectively, the verb "to see, observe, examine" and the noun "nature, quality" or "purity." The basic meaning thus is something like "seeing the nature or quality" without specifying whether it is seeing the nature of oneself (as is often stated in English translations of the term) or seeing the nature of all time and space (which Buddhism teaches us are in no way separable from ourselves).

Awakening and understanding reality are the basis of all Buddhism, not solely of the Zen branch. Within the Zen sects, and between those sects and other branches of Buddhism, though, there are wide differences in views about how awakening may occur and what may follow from a small understanding. The sects that most emphasize an urgent need to experience kenshō seem to have the least regard for the ways in which kenshō alters (or fails to alter) the subsequent actions of the experiencer.

Early in my zazen experience, I asked a priest at Zenshuji, the Sōtōshū temple in Los Angeles, for some books to read about Zen. One of them he loaned me (almost certainly without having read it himself) was Philip Kapleau's *Three Pillars of Zen*. There are two points I remember about that book: one concerning "floating" above the cushion, and the other concerning kenshō, which was called "enlightenment." Luckily I read the one about floating first. The author observed that it is rather common for people with a bit of experience with zazen to feel, during a zazen period, that they are floating in the air above the cushions they sit on. I eagerly absorbed that fascinating note. It was only a few days later, while I was doing evening zazen at home, alone, that I found myself seeming to rise above the cushion. Well, to the extent that real zazen had been going on before that point, it certainly ended in the instant of joyous self-congratulation! When I mentioned the experience to the Zenshuji priest who had loaned me the book, though, his only response was a casual, "Oh, did you?" Wondering about his lack of enthusiasm, I started to think about what had happened. As I tried to remember details of the experience, I realized that given close attention to a statement of that type, a reader has only two responses. Either one soon duplicates, as nearly as possible, the experience that has been presented by someone else, or one mentally vows never in a million years to have even the faintest whiff of such an experience. I say it was fortunate that I read about floating before I read about "having enlightenment," because by the time I read of a second, more profound, experience, I already was somewhat inoculated by my first analysis and sought neither to duplicate nor to avoid what the book described.

Even so, it struck me as terribly impressive that all the people described in the book had reached such heights of Zen practice. I simply finished reading the book, returned it, and by and large forgot about it. Nearly ten years later, someone in the zazen group at Taisōji, the Tokyo temple where I was assisting in services, asked me about the book in general and those kenshō stories in particular. Before answering, I borrowed the book from the questioner and reread the section concerning kenshō. That time, with more training, experience, and knowledge from various sources, my impression was completely different. On that second reading, what most impressed me was the virtually identical descriptions given by a teenaged Japanese female, a middle-aged American male, and a whole group of others having similarly diverse backgrounds. My years of writing and editing experience led me to doubt that there would be that much similarity of described experience if the same group of people had eaten an ordinary meal together and later described their experience of eating. How, then, could a much less public, unshared experience evoke such uniform responses? That was when I remembered the lesson to be drawn from "floating." All the persons in Kapleau's book were members of the same zazen group, with the same priest officiating for zazen and providing both formal and informal Zen instruction. Although details probably were not included in the instruction, it seems certain that quite a clear general idea was conveyed that "if you experience this pattern, you are experiencing kenshō."

The common Zen term for using another's experience and understanding it as one's own is "counting another person's treasure." A classic koan (from the *Sambyakusoku)* tells how Kyōgen spent many years in training under Isan. Despite his best efforts, Kyōgen did not experience even a small awakening. Finally he begged his master, Isan, to tell him the meaning of Buddhist truth. Isan refused, saying it is something that each person must experience directly. Kyōgen left the temple in despair and went to live alone in a mountain hut. After living that way for a long time, Kyōgen one day was sweeping in front of his hut when the broom sent a pebble flying against the stem of a bamboo. At the sound of the pebble striking the bamboo, Kyōgen suddenly awakened. His first action was to return to the temple and present his heartfelt thanks to Isan for being silent, saying it was only through Isan's determined silence that he had the opportunity for the wonderful experience of awakening.

Kenshō comes in many forms, but whatever the form may be, it must be one's own, unique kenshō.

8. What is the difference between zazen and other forms of Buddhist meditation?

The varying branches of Buddhism support a wide range of practices that may be subsumed in the term meditation. Some involve motionless silence; some involve motions, such as walking, or are based on chanting. In all cases, the practices are viewed as a combination of methods leading to awakening and of actions reflecting that awakening.

Zazen, especially Sōtōshū's shikan taza, focuses on experiencing the entire universe as united and discarding the false concept of a separate self. Other forms of Buddhist meditation generally encourage a withdrawal into the illusory self, closing the senses to all that is considered outside the separate self. They do, however, maintain a focus that discourages the flow of discursive thoughts, conceptualizing, and opinions.

Varieties of Buddhist meditation practices include extended chanting of sutras or of a brief phrase of reverence toward a buddha or sutra, visualization exercises, and concentration on the details of bodily actions, among others.

One might think that chanting, whether of an entire sutra or of a short phrase, such as "*Namu Amida Butsu*" (Reverence to Amida Buddha), repeated many times, certainly must halt the flow of discursive thought. If the text being chanted is being read from a page, without having been memorized, any discursive thought that arises will interrupt the flow of the chanting. Once the words (or the actions required to voice those words in that sequence) have been memorized, however, the situation changes. Reading sutras during a memorial service is not really intended to be a form of meditation for the priest performing the service. That is fortunate, because I often find myself thinking "Whatever is that person doing back in the third row?" while continuing to chant a sutra. Most of the time, I can glance at my book, find my place, and proceed without interrupting the chanting. In some cases, I have gone on chanting all the way to the end without looking at the text. This sort of procedure is neither good meditation nor good conduct of a memorial service. It does, however, show how easily our minds can be distracted.

In chanting, any perceptions outside the text being chanted and the self who is chanting (and, if this is a group effort, the voices of the others in the group) are distractions that must be minimized. The effect is of a separate self that perceives only a tightly limited portion of the universe outside that self.

Visualization exercises demand total concentration that excludes everything outside the visualization, which exists as a product of the self. A Tendaishū priest for many years gave monthly lectures that concluded with a short period of zazen. During that zazen, he let everyone become quiet and concentrated then led us through a "visit to the moon." In what seemed afterward to have been quite a long time, although I suppose it really was only a few minutes, each participant visualized the moon drawn on a scroll, then as it appears from earth, and as it appears to a person moving toward it through space. Having finally reached the view provided from lunar orbit, we paused and then gradually descended in the same way we had risen. Any instant of non-attention during the entire process resulted in a loss of the visual pattern reached up to that instant. I found that despite the seeming simplicity of the exercise, maintaining concentration throughout was extremely difficult. Naturally any perception outside the visualization, such as feeling a breeze or hearing the rumbling of a truck nearby, destroyed the required concentration. This exercise and others similar to it demand a total focus on a single thought process to the exclusion of even the sensations of one's own body.

Total concentration on minute details of a simple action, such as taking slow steps, or on the visual components of the scene before one, require a similar level of sustained concentration on what is, in essence, a concept created by the self. No two persons can experience these practices in the same way. No two see the same moon, and the moon that is seen is completely removed from everything in the universe except the mind that performs the seeing.

9. What is the difference between zazen and meditation in other religions or practices?

Most practices that are called "meditation" in English consist of concentration on a certain text. This focus on words and their concepts is directly in opposition to zazen's characteristic of release from words and concepts. For this reason, most Zen priests and lay leaders avoid using the term "meditation" and speak directly of "zazen."

A set of instructions for Catholic meditation, for example, says that a verse from the Bible, a short passage from another religious text, or a religious phrase, such as "Jesus loves me," is a suitable focus for meditation and notes that one should sit erect with closed eyes. The first difference from zazen that we might observe is closing the eyes. We humans have only our sense perceptions to help us toward reality. Of all the senses, sight is usually given the most attention. In fact Buddhist understanding is called "awakening" or "opening the eyes." Yet in the Christian meditation on a text, the sense of sight is used at most briefly, to read the chosen text, and then purposely closed off.

Less obviously, meditation on a text is a method of exploring our concepts. If the chosen text is "God loves me," for example, we first must develop the concepts that we term "God," "love," and "me." Then we proceed to the formulation of concepts for the interrelationships among the first three concepts, and later perhaps we come to concepts extending those interrelationships to additional starting concepts. All this is fine if one wishes to explore and extend concepts. Zazen, however, is concerned with letting go of our concepts and perceiving reality without the veils of concepts and opinions.

One can, of course, sit motionless in an admirably correct full-lotus position while shutting out sensory perceptions and building inward structures of concepts upon concepts. That is not zazen, however.

Other meditation traditions include practices without words, and are thus less focused on concepts, but almost all of them require an attempt to distinguish between "inner" and "outer" spheres, with attention given solely to that defined as "inner." Again, this is a reinforcement of an illusion that zazen is intended to destroy.

10. Do you have to be a Buddhist to practice zazen?

No and yes. The answer depends partly on one's definition of zazen and partly on what, if any, other religion one practices. Taking the definition first, my own definition requires that one comes to zazen as a religious practice, not as a mental exercise, and that one makes a continuing effort to focus on direct reality without reference to one's prior concepts and opinions. It is a matter for deep regret, I think, that the ancient and respected Indian religious practice called yoga now means a type of physical exercise to most Westerners. Starting from the idea of performing physical exercise to improve one's body, it is perhaps *possible* to proceed to a deep religious experience, but that sequence seems highly improbable. In a similar fashion, many Westerners have taken up what they call "Zen" or "zazen" as a mental exercise. The probability of setting out to "improve concentration" or "be less volatile" and proceeding to a life-changing religious awakening seems even less likely than is the case for yoga.

Certainly Buddhism has no patent on sitting erect with crossed legs. The lotus position that is so much a part of all Buddhism is simply a stable posture for sitting on the ground or on a low support. That posture predates Shakyamuni Buddha and has been in continuous use for millennia through much of Asia. Clearly it is not posture alone that creates zazen. It is perfectly feasible to sit in the lotus position while mentally building a whole new social system, for example, or while reviewing information likely to be needed for a school examination. No one, however, would label those activities as "zazen."

The matter of other religions is more complex. For the person of no religion at all, there is no problem. For the person whose religion is one of action rather than belief, there is usually no problem (not being informed on all possible religions, I cannot be completely sure). For the person whose religion is one of belief, and especially of monotheistic belief, there is likely to be a problem.

I once chose as a discussion topic for my Buddhist English class, consisting of young Japanese priests, a U.S. news item concerning a Catholic priest who had also entered the Buddhist priesthood. (In fact, he could not really be properly said to be a Buddhist cleric because the person under whom he entered was not then qualified to accept apprentice priests. That, however, was not part of our discussion.) To my surprise, none of the students found anything strange about the situation. As they immediately told me, it is still rather common in Japan for a person to be ordained as a priest in both Shinto and Buddhism. What had been simply "Japanese religion" until 1868, when the Meiji Restoration revolutionized not only the government but also the culture of Japan, became "Shinto" and "Buddhism" and "Confucianism" by government edict. Until then, both locations and priests were often shared. Both Buddhism and Shinto are religions of action. Adherents performed Buddhist actions (one of which is zazen) in the Buddhist buildings under an appropriately garbed Buddhist priest. The same adherents performed Shinto actions (such as calling on the *kami,* or guardian spirits, for support) in the Shinto buildings under an appropriately garbed Shinto priest who might be the same man or woman as the Buddhist priest. Because the actions are different, there is no perceived conflict. Adherents are not asked to "believe in" either the Buddha or the kami. Both buddhas and kami are simply used as names for aspects of our universe, just as grass and stars and we ourselves are names for such aspects.

The relevance of all this to zazen lies in the perception of reality by the uncolored mind of zazen. A clear mind, experiencing each instant, can experience the oneness of all being and the transience of all phenomena. A mind already dyed with the concept of an eternal being who is independent of the universe must reject that experience or perceive it only through the filters of previous concepts. A Catholic priest, a university professor of spirituality, once discussed zazen and awakening with me. He

had been told that zazen leads to experiencing the unity of subject and 35
object, of self and Buddha. I agreed that his statement is one way of putting that experience into the limitations of words. Then he said that of
course in the next instant, one realizes that self and Buddha are not only
separate but entirely different orders of being. In other words, one who
directly experiences reality in one instant must, in the next instant, reject
that reality in order to return to a preconceived theory. No. Zazen offers
a possibility of seeing reality as it is, free of all our human inventions and
schemes. Quiet sitting, no matter how perfect the lotus posture, is not
zazen if it is a repetition of our normal, human discursive thought,
whether the discourse concerns an eternal being independent of the entire
universe or concerns items to be bought on the way home from zazen.

11. Is zazen good for curing psychological or neurological problems?

Everything nowadays is touted as promoting "stress relief," and zazen is
often part of that promotion. As I noted earlier ("Why do people do
zazen?"), zazen is usually our only experience with being silent and
motionless while awake. That experience, for the mind not closely
engaged in experiencing the moment, works in two directions. Most of
the time, for most of the people, motionless silence is relaxing. It can, in
fact, lead to sleep if an effort at wakefulness is not maintained. Stories
abound of people going sound asleep while sitting upright in zazen posture. One that I heard recently concerned the gung-ho officer of a training temple who regularly exhorted the trainees to reduce their sleep time
in favor of additional zazen time. When the bell for teatime sounded after
zazen, the "sleep less" officer was so deep in sleep that he didn't wake at
the sound. Nor did he when everyone else exited the hall (I grant that exit
and entry are properly performed with minimal noise in any case), nor
when they entered again at the end of teatime. At some point during the
next period of zazen, he finally awoke. Through the entire process,
though, he maintained his posture. Zazen as a sleep substitute or as a
stress-relief measure is another of the many forms of traditional sitting
without really doing zazen.

Provided one stays awake, the other result of an unfocused mind is
daydreams or, in some cases, daymares. Freedom from paying attention to
motion and speech allows the mind time to roam in whatever direction

circumstances may lead. For a healthy person, although the result is not real zazen, it is a pleasant and restful experience. For the already depressed person, however, it is an invitation for the depression to progress from a mild discontent to completely unbearable dimensions. For the angry person, it is a chance for the anger to progress from a mildly miffed level to a murderous rage.

It is for this reason that responsible Zen leaders actively discourage people from doing zazen while they are suffering from some psychological or neurological problem. Attempting zazen in a group may increase the problem. Attempting zazen alone is almost certain to increase the problem. The severe conditions at a training temple for new priests led one trainee I know to enter as a recovering alcoholic but leave there once more drinking. Another trainee entered in noticeably unstable condition and left completely unable to manage the routines of daily life.

No, zazen is definitely *not* good for curing psychological or neurological problems.

12. Will zazen make me feel peaceful?

My master (that is, the priest who accepted me as his apprentice) often asks those seeking a peaceful mind through zazen just where it is they expect the peaceful mind to come from. It cannot float in through the window! He reminds them that unless they have a peaceful mind in the beginning, they cannot have one in the end. Zazen is not, he repeats, about gaining a peaceful mind or anything else. It is a silencing of our normal insistent desires, including that for a "peaceful mind," so that we can perceive reality. That reality, as we discover if we listen and look and use our other senses openly, includes the peaceful mind of knowing the dharma. Chasing after peacefulness, trying so hard to grasp it, is like trying to chase and grasp a butterfly. If we succeed in closing our fingers around the butterfly, we destroy the living beauty that we sought. If, on the other hand, we open a hand and wait motionless, the butterfly may light on that hand and allow us to appreciate its perfection.

A well-known koan tells of Bodhidharma, the priest said to have first taken Zen teachings to China, and his follower who sought a peaceful mind (case 41 of the *Mumonkan,* "Daruma Pacifies a Mind"). When Eka, the follower, begged Bodhidharma to quiet his mind, the master replied, "Bring me your mind and I will pacify it." Although Eka diligently searched for many days, he finally had to admit that he could not find his mind to present it. "You see," said Bodhidharma, "it is already at peace."

The harder we seek for peacefulness, or for anything else, as a product of our zazen, the less possible it is for us to find it. Only by giving up all our notions of seeking and gain can we awaken to the reality that has always been with us.

13. Do you have to go slightly crazy to reach enlightenment?

Point one in response to this question is, as I noted in "What is satori?" that *enlightenment* is an unsuitable term; *awakening* is much nearer to the original term. Point two, also mentioned in the same answer about satori, is that an essential element of the Buddha's awakening is the practice of the Middle Way, following the Eightfold Path. Zen is, after all, a branch of Buddhism. As such, it reveres the Eightfold Path and encourages the best possible observance of the path. No one could conceivably describe mental or emotional illness as an element of the "right views, right thoughts, right speech, right action, right livelihood, right effort, right mindfulness, and right concentration" that constitute the Eightfold Path.

Buddhist leaders starting with Shakyamuni Buddha have exhorted their followers to persistence. Persistence is, indeed, a key factor in "right effort." Persistence, however, is not the same as obsession, and monomania is not a constituent of "right thoughts." Zazen requires both physical and mental health. It takes much more energy and effort than one might think to sit motionless and concentrate on experiencing the current moment. I was amazed at my appetite during the first few sesshin I took part in, when the day was spent almost entirely in zazen. It had seemed to me that with little physical exercise I would have little need for, or interest in, food. Experience proved that the effort of zazen led me to need *more,* rather than less, food than usual.

Wholehearted, persistent effort must balance many factors. It is unique to each individual. Food consumption that is merely a result of greed in one person may be the minimum basic nutrition required for health maintenance in another. Pain that is an element of the moment's experience, a temporary matter until the body adjusts to an unfamiliar posture, for one person may be in itself a cause of physical injury to another. It is not for nothing that the Buddha's teaching is called the "Middle Way."

Hakuin, originator of the koan practice system now standard in Japan, wrote of developing a "Zen sickness" and has been widely quoted as establishing a need to repeat his experience as a prelude to awakening. In fact,

Hakuin viewed the sickness as an impediment to awakening and urged others to use the Taoist healing practice that finally restored his own health and vigor. The very origin of the Buddha's Middle Way was a practice of extreme asceticism, almost to the point of death, that wasted away the body and dulled the mind. It was when he returned to a healthy way of life that he was able to sit in concentration beneath the bodhi tree and awaken to the reality of being.

14. Do you have to like Japanese culture to practice zazen?

This depends on your definition of "Japanese culture." If you think of culture primarily in terms of tea ceremony, flower arranging, calligraphy, and haiku, the answer of course is no. Green tea became popular in Japan as a source of caffeine to keep Zen priests, particularly those undergoing initial training, awake during zazen. Tea ceremony is a much later elaboration of the simple, practical, original cause. Flowers are one of the traditional Buddhist offerings, so priests arrange the flowers to be placed on the altar. Altar flowers, however, are not arranged in the mannered styles taught by popular schools of flower arrangement. Calligraphy is necessary for priests, who must write temporary memorial plaques, the memorial markers representing temples that are offered in honor of a deceased person, and various formal texts. None of these activities are necessary or customary for laypeople.

A wider, more accurate view of "culture," however, reverses the answer. One fundamental element of Japanese culture is an emphasis on group harmony rather than individual opinions. Zazen is one example of that emphasis. As discussed later (in "Can't I just do zazen alone?"), zazen performed in a group is strongly preferable to zazen done by an individual alone. The group practice involves a set of customary procedures that are designed to facilitate zazen for all the participants, even though participants as individuals may find the procedures strange or irritating. Always remembering to turn around in the clockwise direction, for example, lessens the probability of collision with a neighbor. Exiting the zazen hall in sequence by seat location enables a smooth flow of people without traffic jams or pauses for a "You go ahead," "No, you go first" routine.

The difference between promoting group harmony and following procedures as an individual was clearly illustrated by two Western women who were, for a time, lay practitioners at the same Zen temple. The temple rules included walking along a corridor between the main building and the zazen building in a quiet, unhurried fashion. First one of them interpreted that as meaning she should walk as slowly as she possibly could, regardless of the time available before the start of zazen, or of the activity following zazen, and of the number of other people accumulating behind her. Then the second woman, observing that precedent, decided to walk even slower than the first. Competitive slowness set in, forcing everyone else either to enter and leave the zazen building late (and in an irritated frame of mind) or to force a rapid path around each woman, in a violation of harmonious interaction that also led to less-than-tranquil attitudes.

A related element of Japanese culture is an emphasis on form. In zazen this element may be discerned, for example, in detailed rules for serving and eating a meal. One of the functions of detailed form is to focus attention on the matter at hand. In even an informal Zen meal, both server and receiver must pay close attention to the service of food; dropping food in a bowl while wondering how much will be left over, for example, is a sure approach to spilled food, and receiving the food while wondering the same thing is likely to cue the server to provide either more or less than the recipient intended. Food itself is a basis for mannered consumption because Japanese culture places value on the foods that sustain human life through the denial of life to plants or animals.

In both wide and narrow definitions of culture, much of Japanese culture originated in the interactions of the Buddhism of China and Korea with the pre-Buddhist culture of Japan. Inasmuch as interaction had already begun by the early sixth century and Buddhism was accompanied by the introduction to Japan of written language, it is now extremely difficult to distinguish between introduced and preexisting elements. Specific contributions of Zen Buddhism, beginning centuries later, are even more difficult to distinguish from those of other branches of Buddhism. In the wide sense, an appreciation for traditional Buddhist cultural elements is helpful, if not essential, to the practice of zazen.

15. Why are there so many rules about exactly how and when to move?

Even participating in a single period of zazen usually involves a whole sequence of actions that are expected of everyone. Sometimes special groups come to Taisōji for an experience of zazen. Although group members are not likely to participate after the one group visit, and we try to schedule group visits apart from regular zazen services, we coach each group in the normal procedure followed here. It sometimes seems that such rules as which way to turn around and which foot enters the zazen area first serve mostly to confuse newcomers and make them nervous about mistakes.

There are, however, good reasons for even seemingly arbitrary rules of this sort. The instructions for zazen posture are based on observation of physical results of that posture. One overall benefit of the recommended posture is support of the spine and consequently absence of back pain. Eyes focused downward maintain contact with reality while lessening the distractions offered by a large field of vision. Placing the tongue against the hard palate tends to reduce saliva production and the consequent need to swallow.

Other rules allow many people to act with neither interference among themselves nor the need for conversations to sort things out. I have often wished that I could simply assign seats to people attending memorial services in the way seats are assigned for zazen. Then we would not all have to wait while two people engage in a lengthy "Please go ahead," "No, you go first" routine. If everyone always turns around clockwise, neighbors are less likely to bump into each other. If everyone exits in sequence, there is no crowding and no sorting out who goes through the door next.

Beyond practicalities there are psychological effects. Exacting rules require the mind to remain focused on the action of each moment. Focusing on each moment is both the basic action of zazen and the result of continued zazen practice. "Enter the area at the left side, with the left foot stepping in first" is in much the same category as "Maintain at least one car length behind the vehicle in front of you, and increase the spacing as your speed increases." Both require concerted attention to the action in process. Stepping into an area with the right foot instead of the left certainly produces a less-serious result than does tailgating, but the habit of attention to details of our actions encourages many good effects.

Another product of detailed rules is, strangely enough, encouragement of flexibility of mind. Each temple or Zen center has its own variations on the basic standards. Sōtōshū has two head temples, and many small actions differ between the two. When a priest officiates at Eiheiji or a temple following Eiheiji procedures, for example, turning the corners while returning from the altar to the officiating priest's position always is done to the right, turning through the outside of the path. When the same priest officiates at Sōjiji or a temple following Sōjiji procedures, the turn is made inward, to the left. Every Sōtōshū priest must act as officiating priest for one morning at both head temples, as part of the ordination process, so every Sōtōshū priest must learn to act on both sets of rules. That experience surely discourages the idea that there is only one "correct" way to do things.

16. Why do Zen groups use table manners and utensils that ordinary Japanese no longer use?

Eating from one's own set of bowls, unwrapped at the start of a meal and wrapped again at the end of the meal, is a special case of the rules about motions discussed in the preceding answer.

By long-standing tradition, each priest receives a set of bowls, spoon, chopsticks, and bowl scraper, together with napkin, towel, and wrapping cloths, at the time of receiving the precepts and becoming a priest-trainee. These remain with the priest for life. Long-standing traditions do not endure long enough to qualify for that title unless there is something functional about the tradition, and those concerning the eating bowls are no exception.

One fundamental principle of all Buddhism is that the food that sustains our lives is a precious gift not only from the people who raised and prepared the food but from the plants and animals that gave their lives to become an element in our lives. Receiving that gift is therefore a matter for great attention and care. When traditional eating bowls are used, every grain of food is carefully eaten, using the bowl scraper to pick up the final tiny bits, before the bowls are rinsed and packed away, ready for the next meal. The washing is as much a part of the meal as are the serving and eating, so there is no provision for discarding anything except inedible fruit pits.

The reverence granted to the source of our continuing lives dictates that eating be performed with care, in silent attention and appreciation. Even the click of chopsticks is muted. The sequence of setting out and putting away chopsticks and spoon, with chopsticks out first and in second, minimizes clatter. Similar care is taken in each step of preparing to eat, eating, and cleaning up.

Despite all this regulation, there are many small variations used by individual temples. I was exposed to three different sets of instructions for using the bowls, all within the space of a few months of becoming an apprentice. The result, naturally, was total confusion on my part. Finally one day I asked my master which was the correct procedure. He informed me that each procedure was "the correct" procedure for that temple. In fact, he said, if I saw everyone else doing something in what I had been taught was an incorrect manner, for that time and place the "incorrect" way was the right way!

The design of the bowls and related items is part of our heritage from past generations of Buddhists. Our reverent use of them to receive the precious lives of grain, fruit, and vegetables is part of our appreciation for that heritage.

17. Why do I need a teacher and why should the teacher be a priest?

The priest who officiates at a zazen service in Japan is called the *shidōshi*, the master (or teacher) who points the way. Zen priests often warn about confusing a finger pointing at the moon with the moon itself. Nonetheless, someone who wishes to see the new moon in a hazy sky with scudding clouds has reason to be grateful for a finger that points to the area of the sky in which that moon appears. In experiencing the Buddhist teachings, one must perceive and act for oneself—no one else can do that. A finger pointing a direction, though, is a great blessing.

The first and most obvious reason for having a guide to zazen is physical. The guide offers instruction in the physical actions of zazen practice, especially in sitting posture. Home experiments based on reading this or any other book are likely to result in strain on the body, particularly on the back and shoulders. The would-be Zen practitioner then gives up the attempt. An experienced zazen leader can look at your posture and adjust it for balance and stability. The same leader can suggest various less than perfect postures for persons who cannot manage the recommended full-lotus or half-lotus position. During the initial phases of Zen practice, posture is a major difficulty not only for Westerners but for Japanese as well. Not all Zen priests have experience in guiding people with physical difficulties, but those who lack such experience themselves can rely on associated priests for suggestions.

Beyond this physical guidance, the early guidance received concerning the products of zazen is, in my view, likely to determine whether Zen will become a foundation for the acts of daily life or whether it will be only a technique for relaxation or concentration or some other boon that is desired. If zazen is presented as a method of lowering your blood pressure, for example, you very likely will reduce your blood pressure at least during the zazen period, but you are unlikely to go beyond that limited aim. If zazen is presented as a technique of psychotherapy (which in my view is ill-advised, as discussed in an earlier answer), it will be dropped when the need for psychotherapy is reduced or ended. Again there will never come a time of experiencing the dharma as the source of all one's actions.

The zazen leader, especially one who has received training as a priest, can deal with problems that may arise in the course of zazen. Freeing our minds in a large pasture while we sit can, unless close focus on each moment is maintained, lead to daydreams, daymares of the frightening sort, fantasies of all kinds, feelings of anger and feelings of omnipotence, almost anything. The priest who "points the way" cannot prevent such things from arising but can provide guidance in dealing with them and in avoiding repetitions.

One function that seems critical in my own experience is the role of the leader and of a group of other practitioners in preventing the "my zazen" attitude. All phenomena are devoid of self. That is one of the essentials of all Buddhist thought. There is no "me," and nothing thus can be "mine," least of all zazen or sutra chanting or other Buddhist religious practices.

There is nothing magical about a Zen priest. That we are simply humans was the first thing I was told by the priest who later became my master. The study and training required to be ordained (in the real meaning of that term) as a priest in a Zen sect demand sustained effort, if nothing else. They encourage the trainee in observation of self and others, with reflection on what accords with the Middle Way and what does not. Each apprentice is the moral, and in Japan to some extent legal, responsibility of the master. It behooves the master, therefore, to observe each apprentice carefully and to recommend changes in action and attitudes when necessary. All this leads, when things work as intended, to generations of priests who are more-than-usually thoughtful and observant. Few other experiences are as likely to succeed in instilling such habits as is priesthood training.

18. Can't I just read about Zen?

Reading about Zen without any experience of Zen actions is like reading about sex without any experience of sexual actions. And reading about Zen followed by experiments alone is even less likely to have positive results than is reading about sex and experimenting alone.

Both zazen and koan practice demand interactions with at least one leader-teacher-priest, and preferably with an established group of practitioners as well, to set the stage for a meaningful practice. Koan practice without a supervisor is doomed from the very start to be an exercise in imagination and use of the very discursive thought patterns that koan practice is intended to discourage. One conceives a logical, appealing concept, then congratulates oneself on the cleverness of that concept. Alternatively, one finds only illogical, unappealing concepts and berates oneself for the absence of cleverness. Neither result has anything in common with genuine koan practice, and both lead to thought habits that actively oppose those intended.

The case for zazen is more subtle and probably less encouraging. On this topic I can speak from my own experience, although it fortunately was short-lived. Having come upon the Reverend Shunryu Suzuki's collection of dharma talks, *Zen Mind, Beginner's Mind,* I decided to try zazen for myself. Because I had injured both knees, one of which then had only partial flexibility in the knee joint, my first difficulty was with posture. With neither a *zafu* nor a clear idea of what a zafu was, let alone where I could obtain one, I started my attempts by using a bed pillow (much too soft and, after a few minutes, too thin) and sitting on top of my bed (not at all recommended, both for lack in solidity of the sitting base and for the psychological suggestion of sleep). I enthusiastically counted breaths, overlooking the bit about stopping at ten and starting over. Being arithmetically inclined since childhood, I found it perfectly easy to count breaths up to a hundred or more while mentally replaying my irritated conversation with an engineering manager during the afternoon. Luckily I soon realized that whatever was taking place, it was not zazen. Then I located Zenshuji, the Sōtōshū temple in Los Angeles, and started participating in zazen services there.

Most of my zazen time still was spent alone in my home, after a long day at work or at an early hour of the morning. I was tired after work and completely unaccustomed to early rising. Even with the aid of basic instruction and dharma talks from thoroughly experienced priests, it was natural, then, that sitting on a cushion (somewhat more like a zafu than the bed pillow) quickly became "my zazen" and rude interruptions by telephone calls from friends and family at night or birds greeting the morning were resented as disruptions of "my zazen." It was a long time before I started to rid myself of that impediment to zazen. Probably a less passive and solitary beginning would have saved me a lot of later difficulty.

Since that time I have encountered several people whose "just read" beginnings led them into great feats of imagination, of both the hyperstimulated, ecstatic and the completely frightening varieties. One was neither ecstatic nor frightened, but was certain that the Sōtōshū *kanchō* (chief priest of the Sōtō sect) would naturally drop everything to give intensive personal attention to him, a young European who had only six months on a tourist visa in which to reach awakening. He also was certain that both he and the kanchō were, at the time, located at Dōgen's Eiheiji, although in fact he was at Eiheiji's affiliated temple in Tokyo, across the country from the real Eiheiji. When I was called in as interpreter by a priest bewildered at the whole series of misconceptions, it took me three hours that day and more time the following day to convince the visitor of his errors. I have never been certain whether he finally believed what I was telling him or whether he just gave up after awhile. His convictions all stemmed, you see, from what he had read in a book!

19. Can't I just do zazen alone?

The practice of zazen in a group has many advantages over solitary zazen. The most obvious advantage is regularity of time and place. Zazen is both an expression and a source of the awakened mind of Buddhism that shapes the actions of Buddhist life. Zazen thus plays a regular part in the life of a practitioner. Whether that part occurs four times each day or one time each month, it is important that it be an established custom. A group of people must set the specific time and place for each zazen service, whereas a single individual is likely to often change both time and location in response to other activities, feelings, and general convenience. Many people have compared doing zazen to brushing one's teeth: both tend in the long term to have happier effects than those produced by inaction, but neither is likely to fulfill its role if it is performed on impulse, to achieve some immediate benefit. We don't think to ourselves, "I want to prevent cavities, so now I will brush my teeth." We simply brush our teeth when it is toothbrushing time. Similarly, we do zazen when it is zazen time. If toothbrushing required as much time and effort as zazen, perhaps we would need the support of a group for that activity also.

Zazen, as numberless priests have repeated through the centuries, is not an activity performed for a purpose. Indeed seeking some benefit—whether an experience of awakening or a reduction in tension—is likely to prevent the desired result from occurring. With the possible exception of those born in a Zen temple, all of us who practice zazen have some purpose in starting that practice. Dōgen said that zazen is the natural action of the awakened mind that exists in all of us, but we must have some experience of that awakened mind before it can lead us into the "natural action" of zazen. To the extent that we continue to seek some benefit, however, zazen cannot become a natural action.

In addition to offering regularity and stability of time and place, a group provides an atmosphere of support to each member. This support is felt readily in connection with the physical demands of zazen. "If everyone else is sitting motionless, I can remain motionless also" is a common (and helpful) thought during zazen, especially for beginners. Less obvious but more important support occurs in maintaining focus on the moment instead of following some mental discourse. Mental discourse obscures our experience of reality and arouses the 108 desires, or attachments, to which humans are subject. The desires and attachments color our experience, often leading to experiences of joy or anger, both of which are equally unreal. Of course thoughts and feelings arise during zazen. They are a part of our existence as humans. The group, however, somehow aids each member in letting thoughts and feelings go as quickly and easily as they come. Solitary zazen leads easily to dwelling on whatever stray thought or feeling may occur, leading to more and deeper desires and attachments. Zazen is (in those moments when we can experience the moment free of our opinions and concepts) living in freedom from desires and attachments. Both priests and laypeople often remark that the very room in which zazen occurs regularly comes to have a special atmosphere of religious experience. Or perhaps it is just the residue of countless sticks of incense?

It is not always possible to share zazen with a group of people. When the possibility exists, I feel we should take advantage of it with deep appreciation.

20. Why do people bow to their cushions?

They don't. At the beginning and end of zazen, it is customary to make standing bows in the direction of one's own sitting position and in the opposite direction. These bows represent thanks to the other people who are about to do zazen with us and thanks to the other people who have just done zazen with us. Although the zazen hall is likely to have sitting positions facing all four directions, the conventional greetings are simplified by letting one's own side and the directly opposite side represent all the positions in the hall.

What if no one else is in the hall when you enter? Then you bow anyway, thanking the people who may enter later. Even if nobody joins you in your zazen, at the end of the zazen period you may bow to those who have practiced zazen there at other times. It is often remarked that a place where zazen is practiced regularly by a group of people will come to have a feeling of peaceful welcome to all who enter. So we may appreciate all those whose individual phenomena have participated in creating this moment's conditions.

21. Zen is said to be apart from sacred texts, so why do some people chant sutras instead of just doing zazen?

There are many aspects of Zen practice, and sutra chanting is one of them. I had the privilege, several years ago, of participating in a special practice period under the Reverend Kojun Noiri, who has devoted his life to the discovery and practice of Dōgen's rules for the physical practice of Zen Buddhism. In that period, Rev. Noiri told us, our daily schedule was based on Dōgen's advice that one-third of the day should be devoted to zazen, another third to sutra study, and the remainder to work. Sutra study, in this case, included chanting as well as reading silently and listening to lectures. Clearly, then, the founder of Sōtōshū did not neglect the sacred texts.

The statement about Zen being apart from sacred texts means that not *all* the time of a Buddhist priest is devoted to sutra study. There are also times for zazen, and times for work. Zazen itself is not directly involved with sutra study, although it gave rise to an entire literature of its own that relies heavily on quotations from, and allusions to, sutras. "Apart from" in this case means "in addition to" rather than "instead of."

Just as there are many forms of Zen practice, there are many kinds of practitioners. Most members of Zen temples consider zazen to be a special practice for priests, especially during the initial training of new priests. Chanting sutras, on the other hand, is something that is viewed as an activity for laypeople as well as priests. Zazen is preferably a group activity, but sutra chanting may well be done alone. In fact, most sutra chanting by laypeople is performed at the home altar, by the family member who makes the daily offerings of tea, rice, flowers, and incense. In some Zen temples (as in some temples of other varieties of Buddhism), everyone attending a service is expected to participate in the chanting instead of merely listening to the chanting of the priest. Regular meetings for practice in both chanting and writing sutras are a feature of many Zen temple schedules. Writing a sutra in Chinese characters, using a brush and ink, pausing to carefully consider each character, is in itself a form of concentration on the reality of the moment. Those who participate in such activities might well say, "Buddhism is founded on the words of Shakyamuni Buddha, as recorded in the sutras. Why do we need the wordless practice of zazen?"

One of Zen's primary virtues is nondiscrimination, attending to what is here without regard to our personal opinions. Surely, then, a Zen adherent must be the last among all Buddhists to claim that one practice is virtuous and another is not.

22. Can I continue my studies or career while I follow the Zen path?

Buddhism began with four categories of adherents: female and male home leavers (present-day priests), and male and female householders (present-day laypeople). Somehow the latter two groups seem to have escaped the notice of modern Zen enthusiasts. Everyone wants to be a priest, although few of the would-be priests want to undergo the full formal training, or to accept the duties and responsibilities, of priesthood. Whatever happened to Vimalakirti, the householder who expounded the major Mahayana doctrines in a sutra bearing his name, the Discourse of Vimalakirti? What has become of "Layman P'ang," the Chinese Zen layman who was a dharma successor of two famous Zen priests, Sekito Kisen and Baso Doitsu, and whose words are recorded in a book of sayings that has even been translated into English?

Well, to answer the original question, it all depends on what you consider to be "following the Zen path." If you choose to follow the path of the layperson, you not only *can* but *should* continue your studies or career. That is what receiving the precepts as a layperson means: combining a secular life with one's religious activities. The dedicated layperson participates in zazen and other religious activities at a temple or center, as well as at home, but the participation occurs outside study or working hours. Vacations may be spent in intensive religious practice, perhaps. There is no expectation that a layperson will enter a training temple for priests and remain there for months at a time. There is no need for a layperson to do so. There is every need, on the other hand, for the layperson to devote time and attention to the everyday tasks of education or employment. Often laypeople serve, even in Japan, as leaders in some aspects of Zen practice, but they do not carry the full responsibilities of the resident priest. Laypeople observing the precepts demonstrate an awakening, and set an example to others, at least equal to that of priests and in many cases exceeding that of ordinary priests.

If you choose to enter the priesthood (and find a priest who will accept you as an apprentice), you must at the very least interrupt your secular studies or career while taking up the studies and training necessary to achieve ordination. Ordinarily at least two to three years are required to complete the various steps mandated by a Zen sect to become an ordained priest qualified to be resident priest of an ordinary temple, and five or more years are more common. For higher-level temples or higher priestly ranks, the qualification times are correspondingly longer. Life in a training temple is a round-the-clock activity, and the clock often seems to have thirty hours for action and none for rest. Once ordained, the priest is expected to be fully competent to manage a temple and its membership, not only as religious leader but also as finance officer, building and grounds maintenance person, counselor in all of life's difficulties, and community leader, among others. Preparation of someone who typically is under thirty and just out of college to assume all those roles clearly is *not* something to be fitted in along with schooling or outside work. Those who enter a training temple prior to university graduation (usually, in Japan, young women) must generally remain longer than usual before graduating from training. Their combination of secular schooling with Buddhist training is an exceedingly difficult life.

India has a long tradition of reserving one's young adult years for secular life, including maintenance of a home and family. Only when it is time for retirement from that life is it deemed suitable to devote full time to religion. Perhaps our modern world should consider taking that tradition as a model.

23. What should I read about Zen?

The choices nowadays are many times wider than they were when I first became interested in Zen, and the opportunities for Zen practice and Zen learning under competent leaders have multiplied even faster. Reading is now less a matter of necessity than a matter of interest.

Buddhism as a whole, most certainly including Zen, is a religion of actions rather than of beliefs. Unless and until one acts as a Buddhist, reading about Buddhism will be of no more effect than reading about swimming without ever entering the water.

As author of a book about Zen, I suppose it ill becomes me to discourage reading. I really believe, though, that the less reading done during the first year or two of practice, the fewer misunderstandings become firmly implanted in the newcomer's mind.

Zen people acquire the habit of using language in typically "Zen" ways, not to mention the habit of sprinkling their writing liberally with Sanskrit, Pali, Chinese (with two romanization systems), and Japanese (also with multiple romanizations). Much as I deplore such ploys as "translating" from Japanese into Sanskrit, in the guise of providing English (or French or German or what have you), I must confess that I myself often make wildly optimistic assumptions about the Buddhist vocabularies of the general reader.

Even if the language demonstrates exemplary clarity, there are the difficulties inherent in communicating across a gap of more than half a millennium and between cultures that diverged early and widely. The most-accomplished translator can no longer be certain what, precisely, an eighth-century Chinese layman or a thirteenth-century Japanese priest intended to convey in each phrase. That is true even if the translation is from an ancient version of one language to the modern version of the same language.

How likely is it, then, that a reader encountering Zen terms and concepts for the first time will obtain an accurate impression of the original writer's message? A few years of experience in Buddhist actions and a few years of listening to expositions by modern leaders are sure to provide a context for understanding that is at least a little more accurate.

That said, however, there is a place for reading in the life of a serious practitioner. What I would recommend is acquisition of background information before launching into the thickets of Zen writings themselves. For example, a basic text on fundamental Buddhist thought certainly will aid one in later understanding elaborations and extensions of that thought. Similarly a general history of Buddhism and the development of today's Zen Buddhism will give a feeling that human beings, not disembodied mental processes, created the religion we now share.

New books relating to Buddhism in general and Zen in particular are published every year, and scholarship in these areas is growing strongly. For these reasons, I prefer not to name specific books but only to suggest a starting area. By the time you have gained a bit of experience, you will have learned for yourself which types of books will interest you and will support your practice.

24. I want to experience "the real Zen," so I plan to go to Japan even though I don't understand Japanese. After all, Zen is supposed to be beyond words, so I can just feel the meaning, can't I?

There are two sides of this question that must be considered: that of the person asking the question and, more importantly, that of the persons with whom the questioner will be interacting in Japan. Let us consider the questioner's view first.

Early in my own Zen experience, I often was cheerfully assured by Japanese priests that even if I could not understand the language of their lectures, I surely could *feel* the meaning. Not wishing to appear a total dud, I never told them that no, I could not feel the meaning of lectures in a language I did not understand. In fact those lectures probably were the starting point of a terrible habit that plagues me to this day, of simply disengaging my ears from my brain during any long period of subjection to oral Japanese, whether comprehensible (usually the case now) or incomprehensible (as was always the case at the time). The atmosphere created by listeners who *could* understand was a soothing background to either zazen or daydreaming. I quickly learned not to nod off entirely.

What convinced me of the fundamental wrongness of this "feeling the meaning" outlook, though, happened a few years later. Still attending Japanese language school, I took part in a weeklong sesshin at a temple in

Tokyo. A member of a California Zen group—let's call her Eileen—happened to be in Tokyo at that time and also joined in the sesshin. I had enough experience at that temple to know its particular rules and customs fairly well, and thanks to my language school I was able to understand simple statements ("Dust those shelves," for example), so I became Eileen's main interface with the priests and the other laypeople. Still, there were times when Eileen talked with some of the laypeople during a break period while I was not with the same group.

We finished the sesshin with, among other services, a ceremony called *shōsan,* in which priest-trainees present questions to a senior priest. Eileen's experience of that ceremony, which she told me about with great enthusiasm the next day, was certainly much different from mine.

The conversation started with Eileen's remark that she had been deeply impressed with the previous day's installation of temple officers for the next year (the sesshin was held during the first week of December). I asked her what she had heard about installing a new officer; the temple was a large one, also functioning as a training temple for new priests, so it did have a number of full priests resident during the sesshin, but those officers usually serve indefinitely, until they become too busy with their own temples to continue or until they retire from the more-active portions of their duties. It certainly was possible that one was resigning and another being installed, but I had heard nothing about such an event.

Eileen said no one had told her about it, she just *knew* from the wonderful ceremony they performed. As she described that ceremony, I gradually realized she was talking about the shōsan. The first part, in Eileen's version, was when the chief priest asked the new officers questions to be sure their understanding of Buddhism was sufficient for them to perform their duties. Actually that part of the ceremony consisted of the priest-trainees (who were not yet qualified to be temple officers) asking the chief priest questions. It is partly a means of conveying information to the trainees and partly a way of judging their understanding based on the question each poses and the request each may make for additional explanation. Eileen had neatly reversed both the direction and the purpose of the questioning.

Next came what Eileen viewed as a "touching ceremony of continuity" in which, she said, each "new officer" offered incense in token of devotion to the new role, then took a pinch of the incense ash back to put in that "officer's" individual incense burner as a symbol of the continued line of officers serving the temple. It was years later that I finally realized what she had seen to provoke this fascinating, but completely false, story. Each trainee was given a small paper packet of powdered incense to be burned on charcoal in the incense burner. One bows in front of the incense burner, places the packet on the left hand and opens it, offers incense with the right hand as usual, then turns the left hand over, keeping a grip on the packet, so as to drop any remaining grains of incense on the charcoal, and lastly folds the empty paper and stows it in a kimono sleeve for later disposal. It was that final emptying and stowing of the paper that Eileen had perceived as "taking back a pinch of incense ash."

So much for our ability to "just *feel* the meaning."

Now for the people we encounter in this experience. Do you know the Japanese words for "floor rag" and "dust cloth"? About the time you start wiping the lacquered incense stand, or worse yet, altar, with a wet floor rag, there is going to be a crisis in communication. Do you know how to set out, sleep on, and fold away a futon with the neighboring futon on each side less than a foot's length away? Will the serving of each meal be delayed because you don't know which bowl to give the server and how to signal that you have enough food? Even if you have had experience in a Zen center, you cannot know in advance the details of practice that vary for each individual temple. Can you observe your neighbors and adapt to the new situation quickly and accurately enough that your presence will not be a veritable stumbling block to others? Have you ever experienced the heights of frustration engendered by a need to explain something to a person with whom you have no common language? Remember that the temple has not been created simply for your own purposes; it has served others, is serving others, and will continue to serve others long after you leave. Whether your departure is a cause for wide celebration is up to you.

No, you cannot come to Japan with no Japanese-language ability and no relevant background and expect to be anything other than a large impediment to all those around you.

ZAZEN IN PRACTICE

1. What is the lotus position and why should we sit that way?

The lotus position is a sitting posture that originated long before the time of Shakyamuni Buddha and remains in wide use today. The reason for its persistence is the support this posture offers to the spine. Various religious groups have devised metaphysical explanations for the lotus position, but I am firmly convinced that physics outweighs (and precedes) metaphysics in this instance. Sitting motionless for extended periods, typically thirty to fifty minutes, can seriously strain the back unless it is properly supported.

Figure 1. Full-lotus position

The lotus position includes two variants: "full lotus" (in Japanese, *kekka fuza*) and "half lotus" (in Japanese, *hanka fuza*). In the full-lotus position, each foot is placed on the opposite thigh with the tips of the toes approximately in line with the outer edge of the thigh, as shown in figure 1. The full-lotus position offers the best balance and back support of all zazen postures. People who have mastered the full-lotus position are unanimous (in my admittedly limited experience) in pronouncing the

results fully worth the effort needed to train the body to this posture. In the
half-lotus position, one foot is placed on the opposite thigh and the other
foot remains on the sitting surface (floor
or platform), as in figure 2. In both cases
the knees should rest firmly on the sitting
surface, forming a triangle with the buttocks. Please note that the feet rest on the
thighs, not on the knees or calves. Thighs
are wide enough to rest the ankles on and
fleshed enough to accept the weight of the
feet without undue pressure on nerves or
blood vessels.

Figure 2. Half-lotus position

Dōgen's *Fukanzazengi* (General Advice on the Principles of Zazen) says
that in the full-lotus position the right foot should be placed on the left
thigh, then the left foot placed on the right thigh. In the half-lotus position,

Figure 3. Zafu sitting cushion

the left foot should be placed on the right
thigh, while the right foot remains on the
sitting surface. Frequent, prolonged sitting in these positions (especially in the
half-lotus position), however, can tilt
one's hips if the same foot placement is
used every time. Those who sit in the
lotus position for ten minutes a day, or
for forty minutes once each week or month, are in no danger. Those who
participate in a sesshin (see "What is a sesshin, and why do people participate in sesshin?"), however, might be well advised to alternate leg positions
(right over left, then left over right) for alternate periods of zazen. Because
of damage to my knees that predates my
zazen experience, I habitually sit in a single
position and my hips have become slightly
tilted over the years of doing that.

Raising the buttocks on a cushion
makes the lotus position somewhat easier
to achieve and provides a more comfort-
able base than does sitting directly on an inflexible surface. The Sōtō sect
normally uses a round cushion, about 36 cm (14 inches) in diameter and 10
to 15 cm (4 to 6 inches) high, stuffed with kapok (figure 3). Some Rinzai

Figure 4. Interleaved cushions

sects use two thin, square cushions folded
in half and interleaved (figure 4).

    In either case, it is important that the
buttocks rest as far forward on the cushion
as is possible without sliding off. There is
a nerve along the back of the thigh that is
susceptible to pressure. Sitting too far back
on the cushion puts pressure on that nerve
and often results in numbness of the entire
leg. It is customary to sway the upper body

Figure 5. Proper alignment

left and right, then forward and back, at the beginning of zazen to be sure
that the body is centered on the cushion and is upright.

    Usually the back is described as being straight, but really it should be
arched rather sharply forward at the small of the back. A long, straight
object, such as a *kyosaku* (in Rinzai, *keisaku),* held vertically behind the
person in the lotus position should touch the back of the head, back of the
shoulders, and buttocks while leaving an inch or more space at the small
of the back, as illustrated in figure 5. The head should be held slightly
back from its normal position, with the chin tucked in but not inclined

Figure 6. Hand position

downward. All of this provides an erect
spine that can remain motionless without
becoming strained. Dōgen further speci-
fies that the mouth should be closed, with
teeth lightly touching and tongue touching the roof of the mouth. This tends to
decrease the production of saliva. Eyes
should remain open (as do ears, taste
buds, nose, temperature-sensitive nerves, and touch-sensitive nerves), but
it is good to look downward so as to avoid visual distractions.

    Hands rest on the upper foot, with right hand on the bottom and left
hand on the top, palms upward, fingers overlapped so that the second
knuckles of the middle fingers are in line, and thumbs barely touch each
other to form an oval with the fingers and palms (see figure 6).

    This, then, is the ideal posture for zazen.

2. What other positions are acceptable for zazen?

Almost any posture is all right if it is sufficiently stable for motionless sitting without excessive strain. Two of the more common variants are

Figure 7. Burmese posture

"Burmese posture" and "supported seiza." Burmese posture is the same as the lotus position except that both feet and calves remain on the sitting surface, as in figure 7. One foot should be near the body and the other foot, near the opposite knee. The torso is erect, arched at the small of the back, and the head is held back as described for the lotus position. As with the lotus position, it is a good idea to alternate the positions of the legs if you sit in this posture often for more than a few minutes. This is the posture that I normally use because of my damaged knees. I can testify, though, that it does not support the back as well as does the half-lotus position.

The ordinary posture used by Japanese sitting on tatami floors is called seiza, which literally means "correct sitting" (see figure 8). Normally the buttocks rest on the soles of the feet, which are brought together so that the big toe of one foot rests on top of that of the other foot, with

Figure 8. Ordinary seiza

the back held erect. For zazen, though, a zafu or other cushion is placed between the feet to support the buttocks, as shown in figure 9. Because the weight of the body does not rest on the feet, this "supported seiza" is easier to sustain than normal seiza. Some people, especially those taller or heavier than the average Japanese, turn a zafu on edge when sitting this way, thus widening the angle between thighs and calves (figure 10).

 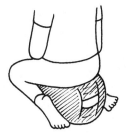

Figures 9 , 10. Types of "supported seiza," the second with the zafu turned on edge

Figure 11. Legs-at-side posture

Another possible position is with buttocks on the cushion, knees side by side on the sitting surface, and calves side by side at an angle backward, as in figure 11. This, however, provides little support to the back and in fact tends to tilt the back, leading to strain.

My general rule for choosing sitting postures is to take care of the back even at the expense of the legs. Aching legs—I have had eons of experience with them!—usually return to normal after about ten minutes of walking around on them. A strained back, on the other hand, can lead to weeks of pain. Early in my zazen experience I eased my legs somewhat by sitting in a way that twisted my back slightly. Unfortunately that twisting was the same as the twisting I had done a few years earlier by incorrect typing posture while writing a long document on a short schedule. My back muscles had cramped so severely that time that I needed daily heat treatments for more than a week. The whole experience was repeated, horrible cramps recurring even when I was not doing zazen, as soon as I replicated the original twisting. It took months to be able to sit once more without fear of those cramps.

3. Can I do zazen in a chair?

"Chair zazen" is becoming a popular trend in Japan, but it poses several problems. The first of those is finding a chair that is exactly the correct height for the individual person. If five people are doing zazen in chairs, there almost certainly should be five different chair heights. The feet must rest comfortably flat on the floor, with the thighs resting on the chair parallel to the floor. Because the back should be in the same posture as for the lotus position, it is usually better to use a stool with no back. If there is a back on the chair, the zazen sitter's back either should not contact the chair back or, in the case of a straight-backed chair, should touch at buttocks, shoulders, and (provided the chair back is high enough) back of the head. Soft cushions distort the posture, but on the other hand there should be some give to the chair seat, just as some give is needed in the cushion used for the lotus position or other on-the-floor positions.

Some priests say that the hands should maintain the same position for chair zazen as for floor zazen. I have found, however, that such a position of the hands can strain the back and shoulders. For those who feel strain, it is better to rest each hand palm down on about the center of the corresponding thigh.

4. What clothing is suitable for zazen?

There are three basic considerations in deciding what to wear for zazen. One is that if you are doing zazen in a group, it is best to conform to that group's apparent style (but more on this later). The other two relate to zazen at home alone as well as in a group. They are the facts that zazen is a religious observance and that zazen is usually done seated on a floor cushion with knees spread far apart. Most religious observances, regardless of the religion, call for a certain conservatism in dress. Clothing that covers most of the body is a good idea, not only for the sake of appearance but also as protection against mosquitoes in summer and chill breezes in winter. Subdued colors, with little or no pattern, are generally preferable.

Given this basis, it is clear that ankle-length slacks in a full cut and soft fabric are a good choice for either men or women. The full cut and soft fabric are needed for zazen's customary spread-kneed position. People often come to zazen meetings in jeans. There are two problems with jeans: the fabric is stiff, so it cuts into the legs where it creases at the back of the knee, and the cut may be rather slim legged, so spreading the knees apart can be difficult. A midcalf- to ankle-length full skirt is also comfortable, especially in winter when the feet can be wrapped inside the folds of the skirt. Most groups, however, would probably frown on a skirt for a man.

The top portion to go with the slacks or skirt should preferably be a quiet shirt or blouse that has sleeves (long or short, but at least so the shoulders are covered), is closed to a point near the neck (though a dress shirt can and should be opened one or two buttons at the neck), and is long enough to go under or over the bottom clothing without gaps.

There is no need for special clothing, and clothing certainly need not be expensive. Just unobtrusive and practical.

Many laypeople in Japan wear traditional Japanese work clothes (called *samu-e* in Sōtōshū and *samu-gi* in Rinzaishū) for zazen. The long trousers, bloused at the ankle and with elastic or cloth ties at the top, are comfortable on one's legs, giving great freedom of motion. The top, made like the top portion of a kimono, has long sleeves bloused at the wrist, a wide overlap in the wrapped front that is secured by ties, and sufficient length to cover the top of the trousers. No one should feel, however, that it is necessary to obtain this clothing. It is enjoying a slight vogue in Japan, and in any case is considered specialized clothing, so the cost is usually quite high here. (Those who are handy with a sewing machine, on the other hand, can make their own sets both easily and inexpensively.)

In the United States, several groups have their own styles of zazen clothing. Such clothing is both conforming and comfortable, so anyone who wishes to maintain a continuing practice in a group showing a specific norm should probably adopt the group standard.

Especially during a sesshin, Japanese laypeople often wear a *hakama,* the long skirt that is worn over a kimono. Those intended for archery are full circles, without the culotte-fashion divided legs of others, making the archery-style hakama especially comfortable for zazen. Either style can be worn. I have often found it hard not to laugh, though, when I see a very solemn Japanese man at sesshin in a black hakama worn with a white dress shirt and no trousers, so the curved, white shirttails peek through the side slits where the hakama front and back come together at the waist. I'd advise anyone wearing a hakama to go all the way and wear a kimono as well.

5. How can I stop thinking?

A widely respected Sōtōshū priest, the Reverend Kōshō Uchiyama, wrote that our thoughts are like our digestive fluids. Both are natural functions, essential to human life, but excessive production of either leads to distress and illness. He also gave a direct answer to the question of how to stop thinking: Cut off your head!

Production of thoughts is a normal and necessary process, but most of us let that process go far beyond the bounds of necessity. In zazen we do not—indeed we cannot—stop all our thoughts. We simply become aware of the arising of a sequence of thoughts and, as a result of that awareness, let go of the thoughts.

For example, perhaps we hear a bird chirp. If we are concentrating very carefully on only this one point at this one instant, we can hear that pure sound and let it go. More often, though, we follow our habitual course of hearing a sound, giving the sound a name, visualizing the source of the sound, remembering other occasions when we have heard the sound, and so on. The bird's one chirp leads us rapidly from this one point and one instant to a whole history of birds we have heard and places we have heard them, perhaps continuing the chain to people we heard birds with and an entire review of our relationship over the years with one or more of those persons. "That sounds just like the birds I used to hear when Grandpa took me to the park. With all the trees and the lake, there were lots of different birds there. And the shade and water made it seem cooler there even in the middle of Buffalo's muggy, airless summer. Sometimes after the park we would go downtown and have lunch at the YMCA cafeteria; I loved being able to choose food from the cafeteria line. But there was that one time when I had scallops there with Grandpa just after I got new glasses, and then got motion sickness on the bus going home. It took me thirty years before I could eat scallops again! That was just before Grandpa gave me a photograph coloring set and . . ." Sooner or later, though, either we become aware of these straying thoughts and return to our focus on here and now or we hear the bell for the end of the zazen period.

It is not all thought that we seek to still in zazen, it is only discursive thought. My ramble from birdsong to photograph coloring is one form of discursive thought. Planning something we wish to do in the future, such as the groceries needed for tomorrow's meals, is another form of discursive thought. Worrying about the possible outcomes of our already-taken actions is yet another.

We cannot create the future; we must wait until it is the present. We cannot re-create the past; it can never return. It is only when we focus on this one point in this one instant that we can experience reality by letting go of our imaginary futures and pasts. To see this instant of reality, we also must relinquish our opinions and preferences. Birdsong or motorcycle engine, sound is simply sound when we hear it with the mind of reality.

6. Why should I keep my eyes open?

The word often applied to Buddhist, especially Zen Buddhist, understanding is satori. As explained previously, this word comes from the Japanese verb satoru, which means not only "to understand" but more basically "to see" or "to awaken." One way of writing these words in Chinese characters, in fact, contains the character for seeing. How can we awaken and see reality with our eyes closed?

In zazen, as opposed to most forms of meditation, not only are we aware of the universe in which we sit, we are more-than-usually aware of our surroundings. To close the eyes means to ignore one aspect of the place in which we do zazen. We cannot close our ears, noses, tongues, our skin surfaces. So why close our eyes?

At the practical level, closing one's eyes while sitting motionless in zazen is a way of duplicating the conditions we normally encounter only while sleeping or almost asleep. It thus tends to cue both mind and body that it is time for sleep. Sleep, however, is not zazen. Keeping the eyes open makes it easier to remain awake and alert during zazen.

Another practical effect is that closing the eyes may encourage the mind to generate random thoughts, then follow those thoughts. We thus are led to entertain ourselves with daydreams, whether happy or horrifying. Simply opening the eyes, on the other hand, engages one's thoughts with present reality.

Although the eyes must be open during zazen, we help ourselves to concentrate by looking slightly downward (at about a forty-five-degree angle) and choosing a single point on which to focus. This limits the visual stimulation we receive. Even during walking zazen (*kinhin*), the eyes should be focused downward, not roaming about.

The system of being alert to sensory perceptions while somewhat limiting the levels and variety of those perceptions (by remaining motionless, in a quiet place, with shelter from the weather) greatly assists us in awakening to our oneness with the universe.

7. Why shouldn't I move during zazen?

In most zazen groups for laypeople, a certain amount of movement during zazen is acceptable. (Priest-trainees are generally required to sit motionless, but the rules imposed on priest-trainees during a brief term of concentrated training are not intended for practice over a long term.) There is much to be said, though, for sitting still. At least we should sit still long enough to examine the need to move. Then if lack of motion will clearly cause some continuing difficulty, we can perform the minimum useful motion in the quietest possible manner.

Zazen is a silent practice and most readily performed properly in a quiet place. Sounds are a natural part of our universe, but a certain amount of quiet is conducive to concentration. As I remarked in "How can I stop thinking," sound easily leads to discursive thought that can wander far away from "this point, this moment." Moving one's body, shifting positions, causes rustling sounds that interrupt the quiet and very likely interrupt the concentration of most of the people doing zazen.

Another practical reason for remaining motionless is the probability of ending in a less-comfortable posture than the one that brought about the motion in the first place. I have found it almost invariably the case that if I shift my feet to relieve pressure on one point or to restore feeling in them, the new position creates worse pressure or promptly numbs the foot that had been all right before. The first part of zazen is the centering of one's body and verifying that one's posture is balanced and erect. That is not preparation for zazen; it is an important part of zazen itself. The complete sequence cannot, however, be repeated during the remainder of the zazen period without distracting both one's neighbors and oneself. The "adjusted" position is therefore likely to be unbalanced.

The more-important reason for sitting motionless is based on viewing reality without our customary distortions of concepts and preferences. The urge to change position reflects not only a perception of unsatisfactoriness related to posture but also an idea that another posture is more pleasant than the present posture. Observing reality means perceiving some sensation (or absence of sensation) without continuing from that sensation to a concept of discomfort, followed by a wish for another posture, followed by a mental image of the comfort that could be obtained through motion, followed by performance of that motion, and very likely followed by the perception of another sensation deemed unpleasant. Instead of building likes and dislikes upon unfounded concepts, we can examine reality through zazen if we examine the sensation without judging it. If there is pressure on a foot, exactly what point of the foot receives the pressure? What kind of sensation occurs? Is it sharp or dull, for example.

The frequent result of such examination is that the sensation slips from the mind's grasp and vanishes. At the very least, a thorough examination while motionless will assist in devising a means to reduce or eliminate the sensation.

Discomfort and pain are parts of the human condition that are familiar to most of us. Few people are able to go through life without encountering them, or even without encountering a circumstance that requires motionless endurance of the discomfort or pain. When I had angiography performed, for example, it was essential to remain motionless not only throughout the incision involved and the test itself, but also for about two hours afterward while the incision sealed itself. The habit of zazen mind was a great assistance to me. So even if we do not manage perfect concentration on reality, the attempt may prove useful at some point.

8. What do I need in order to do zazen at home?

Despite the many reasons for doing zazen in a group with a competent priest or lay leader present, frequent zazen practice usually means doing zazen alone in one's home at least some of the time. Does this mean that each person doing zazen must have a complete Buddhist altar and individual zazen hall? No. The essentials are simple: a reasonably comfortable, supporting place in which to sit and some device for marking the end of the zazen period. All other items are options that may be helpful but are not at all necessary.

First let's consider the zazen seat. Japanese temples have tatami, cushioned by a dense thickness of rice straw under the flexible woven mat, as the base surface for zazen, whether directly on the floor or on a raised platform. Chinese temples, on the other hand, use a hard surface as the base. Few Western homes (or even zazen halls) incorporate tatami, so a base layer is needed to protect knees, ankles, and feet. A thickly padded carpet may serve the same function as tatami. In China, a folded quilt is used for that purpose (Dōgen's zazen descriptions include mention of a futon, or padded quilt, used underneath the sitting cushion). So a quilt or even a blanket is one possibility. Another is a not-very-thick cushion that is large enough for both sitting cushion and knees to rest on it.

Over the base, there should be a sitting cushion to raise the hips at least three or four inches above the base level. A round zafu, about fourteen or fifteen inches (36 to 38 centimeters) in diameter and five to eight inches (13 to 21 centimeters) high, stuffed firmly but not stiffly with kapok, is ideal. The same kind of cushion can be stuffed with fiberfill or foam rubber, but fiberfill becomes compacted after awhile, and foam rubber breaks down, whereas kapok can be fluffed to its original height even after daily use for many years. Another traditional sitting cushion is formed of two rather thin rectangular cushions folded in half and interleaved with each other. (Figures 3 and 4 show a zafu and a pair of folded cushions.) Eventually you will probably want to invest in one of these choices, with kapok filling. More readily obtainable cushions of the standard sofa cushion variety, however, are perfectly usable if they provide the needed height and are not too soft to give adequate support.

Marking the end of the zazen period is not only a practical necessity in most people's lives but also an important mental support. Zazen should have a regular time, regardless of its frequency, and an observable start and finish.

When I started doing zazen, I went to a temple in downtown Los

Angeles twice each week. Very soon I decided to add zazen at home on each of the remaining five days of the week. Having read that training temples normally have zazen first thing in the morning and last thing in the evening, I tried to copy that pattern. The first thing I discovered was that all too often my evening zazen period was abruptly ended by the ringing of the telephone. Shrill, insistent bells are definitely not a happy way to end a zazen period, even if the bells in question sound at a regular time. The kitchen timer that I had pressed into service had a ticking that seemed, in my silent state, to resound throughout the entire house if not the whole neighborhood. And its bell was not all that much quieter than the telephone.

After several months of experience, I gave up the evening zazen at home; even if the telephone and doorbell stayed silent, I was likely to be more interested in going to sleep than in concentrating on zazen. For morning zazen, when the need to get to work made some sort of timer mandatory, I took the suggestion of a priest at the temple and started burning short sticks of incense at a position within range of my peripheral vision but not at the focus of my eyes. Stick incense burns down at an even rate, consistent from one stick to the next. Indeed the burning of stick incense was used as an early form of clock in ancient China and Japan. Even now if I am doing zazen alone, that is the method I use. Looking at a clock or watch, as I do when I am marking the time for *other people's* zazen, can easily become a distraction from the zazen itself. The incense level is somehow less obtrusive, I think. Alternatives include kitchen timers, preferably without audible ticks and with less-than-fire-alarm sounds when the time has expired; alarm clocks, again of the subdued variety; and any household appliance that can be set to turn on with an audible click at the end of a time period or at a set hour and minute. The quiet engendered by zazen means that any loud, sudden sound will cause a much greater than usual reaction, so gentle cues are easier on one's heart rate and blood pressure.

Even if it is not used as a timer, incense is a helpful option in my experience. The scent of the incense becomes associated with the practice of zazen, thus helping the mind to settle into alert concentration on the moment.

Those who wish to follow the Japanese custom of a home altar, where one dedicates sutra chanting and makes the traditional Buddhist offerings, will need a Buddha statue or picture and offering utensils. There is no need for the cabinet generally used in Japan; those are expensive in Japan and difficult to obtain elsewhere. My own home altar is the top of a small chest of drawers. The traditional offerings consist of a candle, flowers, rice, tea, stick incense, and powdered incense. The powdered incense is burned on either a small piece of charcoal or a bundle of short pieces of stick incense. Hot water is considered a form of tea, and is often used as the tea offering. Coffee drinkers might offer coffee instead of tea. In the likely event that rice is not a daily essential for you, your own staple food might be substituted. The rice and food offerings normally are made in small containers specially intended for that purpose, but ordinary cups and dishes are fine.

Not long after I began chanting (in Japanese) the Heart Sutra (Maka Hannya Haramitta Shingyō) after my morning zazen, I bought a Buddha statue and what I thought of as suitable utensils for offerings. One that I was particularly pleased with, found in San Francisco's Japantown, was a small brass bowl on a round cushion. The incense burners I had seen were much larger and quite elaborate. So I thought this "incense burner" with its "insulating cushion" was much simpler and nicer, not to mention smaller. Instead of a layer of ashes with charcoal on top to burn the powdered incense, I used solid cones of incense. What little ash was created stayed in the bottom of the bowl as insulation. A few months later, a Sōtōshū priest on his way back to Japan happened to visit me, and I asked him to chant the Heart Sutra with me and to say the dedication for that chanting. He promptly approached my home altar (on top of an armoire at that time), lit the candle and a stick of incense, then started searching for something. What he was looking for was the striker to use with my gong—and he was astonished to notice, during the search, that there was something white in the bottom of the gong. My "incense burner" was a gong!

Well, eventually I acquired a "real" incense burner, a bag of incense ash, and a box of small charcoal squares. The gong reverted to being empty and struck. Nevertheless, it had been a very nice incense burner. There is nothing disrespectful or "wrong" about using what is available at hand, and no need to purchase expensive equipment from Japan. What is important is your action in offering light, flowers, incense, food, and sutra chanting, and your dedication of all of those to the furtherance of the Buddha's way.

9. How long should I do zazen at home?

People who start zazen at a temple or Zen center tend to attempt the same time period at home that they have known in the group meetings. Usually this is forty to fifty minutes for each period of zazen. I believe that such long zazen periods at home are not a good idea, for several reasons.

When I first started doing zazen at Zenshuji, the Sōtōshū temple in Los Angeles, the zazen period was forty-five minutes. On Monday evenings, there was a short period of walking zazen (kinhin) after the first zazen period, then another period of zazen. On Saturday mornings, one period of zazen was followed by morning sutra chanting in the main hall of the temple. It was very painful for me to sit on a cushion on the zazen platform. The aftereffects of surgery on one knee, and the continuing effects of arthritis in both knees, made it impossible for me to get my knees down to the platform even in Burmese posture. So when I asked about zazen at home and one of the priests suggested five to ten minutes, I was greatly relieved. Despite that encouraging suggestion, I felt that "really" a much longer time would be "better." In the years since that time, I have come to believe that five to ten minutes truly is a suitable duration for solitary zazen at home. Twenty minutes is perhaps the longest appropriate duration for such zazen.

One reason for short zazen periods is the difficulty most of us have in fitting another lengthy item into our already-crowded daily schedules. Zazen should not be a special occasion. It should be a normal, regular part of daily life—or weekly or monthly life. Both physically and mentally, we adapt to zazen better as part of a standard routine than as a practice to be debated or pushed into a time normally used for something else. I can certainly testify that it is easier to reserve ten minutes each morning for zazen than it is to reserve nearly an hour each morning.

Another reason is our attention span. Maintaining the alert focus of zazen requires a surprising amount of effort. Trying to make that effort for ten minutes is much more likely to succeed than trying to do so for forty minutes. I have often found myself, at the start of a forty-minute zazen period, even one with other people present, half-consciously deciding that I can daydream for a few minutes before settling down to real zazen. The result, of course, is forty minutes of daydreaming instead of zazen. Setting a short time limit makes zazen precious; we don't want to waste an instant of that short time, so we work hard at staying alert and focused.

Somehow the presence of other people, all making the effort required for zazen, seems to help each individual to continue in the effort. I suppose we feel that if everyone else is concentrating, we must individually hold up our part of the group effort.

Being in a group also decreases the tendency to grasp zazen as a personal possession. It is very easy, when sitting alone and especially doing so for an extended period, to start believing that the whole universe should stop and devote itself solely to "my zazen." The neighbor who breakfasts to radio music becomes a "rude enemy." Even the morning song of summer's cicadas comes to be heard as an interruption to "my zazen." As do the heat or cold, the vibration of a heavy truck passing by, and other sensory inputs. The instant when zazen turns into *my* zazen, it is merely an unusual sitting posture while we pursue our usual deluded concepts. The very things that we then perceive as "interruptions" are the phenomena of the instant, the phenomena we seek to experience in each instant so as to know reality. That knowing of reality in the instant is the meaning of zazen.

10. How can I know it is time to lengthen my zazen periods?

As the answer about the length of zazen periods indicates, the first thing to consider is whether there is any reason to lengthen your zazen period. Assuming the answer is yes, perhaps because you have difficulty in adjusting to the longer zazen periods when you are at a temple or in a group elsewhere, it is mostly a matter of being alert to your own condition.

Perhaps your body will not shape itself into a stable position. This was the case for me when I could not lower my knees to the sitting surface. It is probably more effective in this case to carry on the adaptation effort on two fronts if possible: increasing the number of zazen periods and lengthening the periods. When one zazen period of five minutes each day feels reasonably comfortable, try two periods of five minutes each, preferably several hours apart. Then when that is not too difficult, try one period of ten minutes and leave the other at five minutes. And so forth. During all of this your body will teach itself how to sit. You can also carefully observe which areas seem to be problem points, then try adjusting your posture a bit so as not to strain those problem points. Perhaps you can place a small handkerchief or towel beneath an ankle bone that is carrying too much weight against the floor.

If you find your mind cannot remain alert after the first minutes of zazen, don't try a great leap in zazen time—repeated failures will only discourage you and may even reinforce the pattern of inattentiveness. When you can remain alert for five minutes, try to extend that alertness to seven minutes. After seven-minute alertness has become consistently possible, aim for nine or ten minutes. Remember, though, that no one stays uniformly alert and focused for forty minutes or more. Zazen is a process of focus followed by drifting thoughts followed by awareness of the drifting and returning to alert focus.

In the case of either physical or mental difficulty, you will probably find that what you can manage for about thirty minutes alone, you can manage for forty or fifty minutes in a group.

11. How can I do zazen while I am parenting a young child?

It seems to me that this question often arises from a misunderstanding of the role of zazen in daily life. Doing *anything* while parenting a young child is more difficult than doing the same thing without the complications engendered by the child. Zazen is no different from the rest of one's regular activities in that respect.

First, some suggestions, then I'll take up the matter of misunderstandings.

Infants and toddlers often need to be held for awhile to go to sleep. What better time for a parent to have a few quiet minutes for zazen than the time between the child's quieting and sound sleep! Probably the parent's posture will not be the usual zazen posture, but that is not important when the period of sitting is brief. The child's quiet may well help the parent to concentrate, and the parent's concentrated zazen may communicate a sense of peace and security to the child.

Brief zazen periods at home probably will be the main form of zazen for those with very young children. It is a matter of finding a time when five or ten minutes can be taken in reasonable assurance that they will not be interrupted. As with anyone doing zazen at home, parents are likely to find that early morning is the most suitable time. Provided, of course, that an alarm clock does not wake child together with parent. A child's nap time offers another chance.

Depending upon the circumstances of the group, it may be possible for children to accompany parents to an outside zazen meeting and stay in a separate room where they can play freely without disturbing those in the zazen room. Group members can take turns caring for the children. Child care is not zazen, but it can be a wonderful Buddhist practice of a different sort.

Again, the parent who wants to attend a zazen meeting (and it is good to sit with other people at least once a month or so) can arrange for the other parent, or a relative or friend, to stay with the child for that time. Parents can take turns, alternating zazen attendance with child care.

Attending a sesshin is likely to prove very difficult while one is parenting a young child (or even a school-age child). Sesshin, though, is not a necessity. Many people have a wonderful zazen practice without ever once doing a sesshin.

This is where the misunderstandings come in. Many Western people, and some Japanese as well, seem to think that there cannot be any Zen practice without frequent attendance at a three- to seven-day sesshin, or believe that the only "real" zazen is that which takes place in a temple or Zen center. Nothing could be further from the truth! Real zazen is zazen that engages the entire body and mind of the person sitting, regardless of where, when, and for how long that condition may be obtained. Five minutes a day at home is likely to be a much truer practice than a sesshin once a month with no zazen between times. The pattern of monthly sesshin was developed for training new clergy in a short time (typically a year or two). It is not expected that resident priests will desert their temple members every month or that laypeople will halt their normal lives to act as priest-trainees every month.

12. What is a sesshin, and why do people participate in sesshin?

A sesshin is a few days of concentrated zazen practice; during a three- to seven-day period, participants spend almost all their time in zazen, using twelve hours or more each day for zazen itself and remaining in the zazen hall for periods of sutra chanting and meals. To the extent allowed by a particular temple's facilities, participants even sleep in their zazen locations.

The two Chinese characters used for the word sesshin represent the verb to catch or to capture and the noun for mind or heart. The uninterrupted devotion to zazen throughout the day and night helps concentrate the mind so it can experience reality. The efficacy of sesshin for this concentration is partly caused by the unusual nature of the experience. It demands a rigorous attention that cannot be sustained through the multitude of daily concerns in ordinary life. One factor aiding in concentrated zazen is the instruction offered by the priest directing the sesshin during both informal comments and formal lectures. Even a single sesshin will often bring about a marked deepening of religious understanding.

Training temples for new priests, which form the reference point and model for most Western Zen centers, hold a sesshin once each month in principle. January and August are months in which local temples have major duties, so these months are often excluded from the schedule. The priest-trainees are allowed to return to their home temples to assist in the New Year's activities and in summer's primary memorial season, Obon. In addition, most of Japan is extremely cold in January and extremely hot and humid in August. Neither condition aids in exclusive focus on zazen, particularly the breathless, wet heat of August.

Training temples, though, are a place in which a priest must be shaped for life during the brief span of a year or two. Activities in such temples are necessarily at great odds with the activities of normal temples serving their local members. Funerals, memorial services, community service, counseling, and the many other duties of an ordinary resident priest rarely can be combined with monthly retreats into a zazen hall.

There are two primary sesshin times each year: the first week of December, leading up to the dawn of December 8, which Japanese tradition says is the time when Shakyamuni Buddha first reached awakening under the bodhi tree; and the week leading to February 15, the date on which Japanese tradition says that Shakyamuni Buddha entered nirvana. If an ordinary temple holds sesshin, these are times when it will be observed in most cases. The length of the sesshin is often reduced in ordinary temples.

Typically, the schedule for a Sōtōshū sesshin may be something similar to this:

3:00 A.M.	Wake up
3:20–6:00	Zazen (including walking zazen and brief breaks), tea, and morning sutra chanting
6:00	Formal morning meal, followed by cleaning period
7:50–11:00	Zazen (including walking zazen and brief breaks),

tea, and lecture

11:00	Formal midday meal, followed by rest period
1:00–4:00	Zazen (including walking zazen and brief breaks), tea, lecture, and evening sutras
4:50	Evening meal, followed by rest period
6:20–9:30	Zazen (including walking zazen and brief breaks), chanting of General Advice on the Principles of Zazen

9:30 Go to bed

Tradition calls for omitting baths and shaving during the sesshin, so it is with enormous pleasure that participants greet the opportunity to bathe between the conclusion of the sesshin and the sutra chanting that marks the Buddha's awakening or death anniversary. The strong-smelling liniments used to ease knee joints seem, by then, to have penetrated every cell of the body and every thread of clothing. Release from the rigorous schedule, though, sometimes leaves participants briefly feeling directionless, unready to take up the tasks of everyday life once more. When daily life is resumed, it is resumed with a reserve of attention, devotion, and caring that has been accumulated through the sesshin.

13. Every Zen temple in Japan has daily zazen, doesn't it? How can I find one to attend?

Except for training temples, very few Zen temples conduct daily zazen. Ordinary temples are devoted to serving their member families and the community. Member families are rarely interested in zazen, viewing it as an ascetic practice performed by priest-trainees. The demands on a resident priest's time often mean keeping late hours that make evening zazen impossible and early morning zazen extremely difficult.

The usual result is that zazen services are held once a month, if at all. More enthusiastic priests may offer zazen once a week. Anything more frequent than once a week is quite rare. It must be remembered that Buddhism is not a proselytizing religion. There is no program in Zen temples for actively seeking new people to take part in zazen. The basic attitude is that when someone is ready for zazen, that person will come to the temple for zazen.

One solution to the problem of finding a zazen service at a temple in Japan is to consult the Japan National Tourist Organization. Several of the temples that are able to offer zazen to newcomers, especially to new-comers who are not fluent in Japanese, are listed in the resource pages maintained by that organization. There are offices in large cities and tele-phone information numbers. After you obtain information about any temples they may list in your general area, including the dates and times for zazen, you can start exploring those temples.

Some travel guides provide information on zazen meetings, but I have found the guides to be unreliable. Not only are they often out of date, but several seem to have copied information from other guides with no attempt at verification. I have more than once been shocked to find that a recently published travel guide presents information about my zazen meetings that is more than ten years outdated. Do not be surprised, then, if a temple has changed the zazen schedule or if the English- (or French- or German-) speaking priest is no longer there.

Many of the foreign-language newspapers published in Japan provide space for announcements of events that may interest their readers. Those announcements are guaranteed to be up-to-date and include principally (if not entirely) events for which the primary language is that of the news-paper, whether English, Portuguese, Chinese, Korean, or other.

The head temples or administrative headquarters of Zen sects can sometimes provide helpful information, as can the Bukkyō Dendō Kyōkai, a pan-Buddhist organization located in Tokyo that publishes an informative series of books on Japanese Buddhism. Local cultural or tourist organizations are other possible sources.

Perhaps the simplest approach, especially if you want to remain within your home neighborhood, is to devote some time to looking at the temples nearby. Note those that identify themselves as being part of a Zen sect. Perhaps there may even be a notice board by the gate showing the schedule of regular temple activities.

However it is that you home in on a temple where you may be able to join a zazen group, the first approach is very important. Westerners should make every attempt to enlist a Japanese acquaintance to aid in the first request for information. This is not just a matter of your Japanese language skills; when someone at the temple looks at a Western face at the door, or hears a Western-accented voice on the telephone, the first reaction is likely to be a panicked thought that communication will be impossible because the temple person cannot speak English. The sight of a Japanese face at your side, or the soothing tones of a Japanese voice on the phone, will do wonders for the peace of mind of the person you wish to query. For much the same reason, try to persuade a Japanese acquaintance to accompany you the first time you go to a zazen meeting. After the first time, if you can manage at least a little Japanese and if you show some familiarity with Zen and Japanese customs, everyone will relax and you can be accepted on your own.

After you have participated in zazen at one temple a few times, you can decide whether that temple's approach to zazen is comfortable for you to accept. If you feel truly out of step with the priest or the other participants, it probably is best to start the process over again and try to find another temple. Remember, though, that conditions and customs in Japanese temples have remarkably little in common with those in Western Zen centers. The Japanese temple customs are shaped by several centuries of continued existence, if not of the one temple you attend then at least of the sect that temple belongs to. Adjustments will in most cases be solely on the side of the Western participant. Making adjustments under such conditions can be considered another excellent form of Buddhist practice.

14. How can I find a zazen group outside Japan?

When my interest in zazen was first aroused, I discovered a Sōtōshū temple (because the book that caused my interest was written by a Sōtō-shū priest) in Los Angeles by the simple process of consulting the yellow pages of the telephone directory. The directory for the suburban area where I lived and worked had no Sōtōshū listing, but the main Los Angeles directory did. So that is where I went, after calling to ask about zazen meeting times and whether instruction was available in English. It is, however strange it may seem, a practical way to start your search.

Internet usage is more developed in the West than in Japan, so another way to locate possibilities is by an Internet search using, perhaps, "zazen" and your general location as keywords. Or you can subscribe to a mailing list on a Zen-related topic and either pose a question about zazen groups in your area or just watch for mention of such groups in the mail on the list.

Community centers may provide news of groups in your town, or a Zen sect headquarters in your region may have listings.

Once you find a possible zazen group, the first thing to do is to visit a few of its meetings. If the group seems competently led and generally attuned to the kind of Zen practice you seek, your search is over. If you have serious reservations about the group or its leader(s), visit another group. Many zazen groups are quite sensitive about "shopping around," so it probably is best not to converse about other groups you have visited. If you sincerely try three groups or more and are not satisfied, probably you have set up your own notions of what a zazen group should (or should not) be. The start of real zazen in that case is to let go of your own opinions and just concentrate on the zazen of facing one instant's reality.

Even a group with a clearly unsuitable leader (meaning one with little or no knowledge of Buddhism or one whose personal or professional conduct is clearly contrary to the spirit of the precepts) can provide a sustaining environment for zazen when the individual member's practice remains focused and pure. (This is not, by any means, a recommendation that you practice under such a leader, unless no other group is available.)

15. Why do Zen priests hit people with a stick during zazen?

Whenever zazen is shown in a Japanese movie or television program, the loud slapping sound of a flattened stick on a shoulder or back muscle invariably resounds within seconds of the beginning. Judging by films and television, we might assume that Japanese zazen is a continuous round of hitting other people or being hit. In real life, though, this occurrence is normally limited to training temples for new priests. Laypeople who participate in zazen are more likely to encounter that stick as something held silently against the back to allow the sitter to feel the correct, straight-backed posture.

The stick is called a kyosaku (in Sōtōshū) or keisaku (in Rinzaishū and Ōbakushū). Although the pronunciations differ, the Chinese characters with which the word is written remain the same, as does the object itself except for some difference in length. About a meter long, the kyosaku is thick and rounded at one end, thin and flat at the other. The priest holds the rounded end with both hands while patrolling the zazen area. If someone raises hands in the gesture of respect, the patrolling priest will go to that person with the kyosaku. In Sōtōshū, everyone normally does zazen facing the wall, either on a raised platform or on the floor. The priest stands or kneels behind the requesting person, bows to that person, gently taps the kyosaku on the right shoulder muscle to give notice, then, while the receiver leans forward just a little and tilts the head to the left, the priest swings the kyosaku rapidly up and back to the shoulder muscle. Correctly done, this delivers a very loud, stinging slap without any bruising or any pain beyond the first moment of the slap. This concluded, both the patroller and the receiver bow in appreciation of each other.

In Rinzaishū, with people facing inward toward the center of the room, the patrolling priest is visible so no notice is necessary. As the patroller bows, the requestor bends forward with head touching the sitting surface and one forearm flat on the surface while the other hand is tucked into the opposite armpit. This raises one shoulder. The patroller slaps the keisaku on the large muscle at the back of the raised shoulder, usually striking twice quickly, then pauses while the receiver changes position to raise the other shoulder and strikes that muscle twice. As in all sects that practice zazen, the giver and receiver of these slaps bow to each other at the conclusion.

Why would someone want to be struck? One reason is a feeling of sleepiness. The sound and the stinging sensation bring the receiver's mind back to alertness. In fact the sound thoroughly awakens anyone else who may have been drowsy. I encountered another reason fairly early in my zazen experience. A few years earlier, I had foolishly typed a manuscript sitting with my upper body twisted so I could look at notes on my desk while using a typewriter that was perpendicular to the desk. The result, after two or three days of constant typing, was severe spasms in my back muscles. I had thought my back was fully healed from that experience until I started having spasms—fortunately much milder ones—during zazen. Apparently I was sitting with my body slightly twisted. When I asked all three of the priests under whom I did zazen at that time, though, they could not see what was wrong with my posture. Higher and lower sitting cushions failed to help. The spasms grew more frequent. Finally one priest, who had left a training temple only a few months earlier, suggested that I ask for the kyosaku. The muscle that is slapped somehow causes a reflex straightening of the back. (A friend later remarked that it is the exact spot where her doctor used deep massage to ease her back pain.) We tried, and he was correct! The spasms magically vanished in the instant of the slap. After some time, my back learned to straighten itself and I became able to do zazen without

muscle spasms. The same reflex straightening can be a help to someone
who habitually sits with a slumped, curved back and cannot retain erect
posture through the zazen period. Posture is not a matter of aesthetics or
custom: it is a method of preventing back trouble, so it is important to
learn and use the correct posture.

The name of the stick has interesting associations and derivation. The
first character means precept, exhortation, instruction. The second does
not, as one might expect, mean stick or something similar; instead it
means rope or whip. The entire expression, keisaku, has been used to
mean spurring a horse on to greater speed with a whip (or, one assumes,
a piece of rope). From that came a use in literature to designate an important passage that animates the whole text or a literary work that imparts a
profound inspiration. From those meanings has come the Zen meaning of
"awakening stick," in which "awakening" means both from literal drowsiness and from our human delusions.

16. What if my foot goes to sleep?

The main problem with a foot becoming numb during zazen occurs at the
end of the zazen period: it impedes getting up. When people do zazen in
a special hall with raised platforms to sit on, it is not uncommon to see
someone start to stand and instead fall down. Even rising from the floor
with a numbed foot can be unstable and possibly lead to injury.

The most important response to a numbed foot, therefore, is being
aware of the condition and using great caution in moving about until feeling is restored to normal. If you are sitting on the floor, placing your feet
gently down on the floor then squatting over them may help to restore circulation quickly. If you are sitting on a platform, it is a good idea to move
each foot in a circle before attempting to stand up; the motion will warn
you if a foot is numb.

Usually a numb foot is caused by sitting in a slightly unbalanced posture, possibly caused by using a cushion that is either higher or lower than
you are accustomed to using. If you start to sense a numbness during
zazen, the slightest movement of your foot—even just tensing the muscles
without any motion—may restore feeling. In most groups, it is acceptable
to adjust your position slightly after making a small bow with raised
hands, palms together, to ask your neighbors' pardon.

Although this is a common problem for people just beginning to do zazen, it generally is not a serious or long-continuing matter. The body seems to learn how to adjust itself to an unfamiliar posture and corrects for undue pressure. If you have consistent trouble for some time, tell the priest responsible for your group and ask that your posture be closely observed and corrected.

17. What should I do when my legs hurt?

Pain comes in many varieties. The first response should be assessment of the variety you are experiencing. A slight pain needs little, if any, reaction. Severe pain calls for countermeasures. As with a foot going numb, pain in the legs generally lessens as the body adjusts itself to a new posture and new demands on muscles and tendons.

One fact to bear in mind regarding sore legs is that most measures to reduce strain in the legs cause strain in the back. Leg strain usually is much more easily remedied than back pain, so simply waiting for the end of the zazen period may be the most appropriate response. My own rule of thumb, developed while the aftereffects of surgery had left me with only partial mobility in one knee, is that any pain that goes away within ten minutes of walking is a pain that can be simply ignored. Until the end of the zazen period, once your mind is focused on a sensation of pain any-way, giving complete attention to the sensation—precisely where is it located? precisely what kind of pain is it?—often results in the pain slith-ering away under scrutiny.

Ankle bones may be subject to pain from contact with a hard surface. This can be remedied by inserting a folded handkerchief under the suf-fering bone. Similar slight adjustments, made at the start of a new period of zazen or even during a period of zazen, often relieve pain in a limited area.

Pain that continues through a period of walking zazen (kinhin) calls for a change of posture for the next period of zazen. Reverse the positions of the legs, so that the one that was on the inside is outside and vice versa. If you have been sitting in the full-lotus position, try half lotus, and if you have been sitting in the half-lotus position, try Burmese style or supported seiza. Despite Dōgen's instructions to place the right foot on the left thigh before placing the left foot on the right thigh in the full-lotus position, anyone doing zazen for extended periods of time is well advised to alternate the positions of the legs. Because of my knee injuries prior to starting zazen, I habitually sit in one position, and my hips have tilted somewhat over the years so that one leg is effectively shorter than the other. Alternating positions prevents development of such a tilt.

Continuing pain may require that you use less-stressful postures, possibly using "chair zazen," reduce the length of your zazen periods, or even halt all formal zazen for a time. Remember that true, completely focused zazen for one minute means more than hundreds of hours of mere sitting without focus.

18. I often feel very warm during zazen, even if the room is cool. Why does that happen?

For some people, zazen shifts the circulation of blood toward the skin, resulting in a feeling of warmth and a reduction in internal temperature. The same kind of circulation shift occurs, I recently learned, at the beginning of sleep when our bodies seek to cool down. Perhaps the shift is somehow triggered by the zazen posture, or (more likely, in my own unscientific view) perhaps by the tendency toward slower breathing as zazen proceeds. It is far from being a universal experience but is reasonably common. The only meaning that this experience holds is that if you have it a few times you may want to choose somewhat cooler clothing for zazen than for, say, sitting at a desk.

Before Taisōji erected a new building with windows that actually seal out the wind, and with central heating, winter zazen often produced an epidemic of chattering teeth at the start of walking zazen or sutra chanting. People whose circulation patterns had kept them comfortable through the zazen period suddenly shifted to less surface circulation and began to feel the winter drafts.

This phenomenon is part of the reason for scheduling a rest period after each meal during sesshin. Soon after I became a priest-trainee, while I was still attending a Japanese-language school, I participated in the February sesshin at a nearby temple. The midday meal was late one day, and it turned out to be "curry rice," a curry sauce combined with white rice. There was a funeral service at the temple that day, so the priests who ordinarily would have prepared the meal were instead assisting with the funeral. Immediately after eating, we returned to zazen, starting at the regularly scheduled time but without any rest period. Soon my stomach began to feel as though I swallowed a large lump of lead! Circulation concentrated in the skin means low circulation in the digestive system. It was an experience I have recalled as a warning each time I schedule a round-the-clock zazen activity.

19. What should I do when I itch during zazen?

This question arose one day after a zazen meeting conducted by the priest I apprenticed to. It was summer, which in Tokyo means hot and humid, so itchiness was widespread even without the abundant supply of hungry mosquitoes. In answer he told about his own experience as a priest-trainee. On a summer evening, he suddenly felt the sting of a mosquito bite, followed immediately by itching. Acting on reflex, he reached up and scratched the bite. At that motion, the priest conducting the zazen shouted at him, and he returned his hand to its proper place. Later, though, he asked that priest why he had shouted. We are told to follow our natural feelings, my master said, and what is more natural than scratching a place that itches? The senior priest replied that he shouted not because of movement during zazen, although that is forbidden for trainees, but because scratching once only increases the itching and soon the entire experience is one long sequence of itching and scratching. Worse yet, the motions and their sounds are perceived by the others doing zazen. This reminds them of their own mosquito bites or other itches. Soon half the participants are busy scratching instead of busy concentrating on the moment.

How to prevent such an occurrence? Well, keeping mosquitoes away from the zazen area is one method, of course. For the itching person, however, that measure comes too late. An itching sensation can be dealt with in the same way as a minor pain: concentrate on the details of the sensation until it vanishes.

Much the same reasoning applies to moving about during zazen for other reasons. The wish for motion, including scratching motions, is an attachment, a desire. It involves our opinions about "comfortable" and "uncomfortable." While we are thinking about desires and opinions, we cannot observe the reality of the moment just as it is.

20. What should I do if I feel sick during zazen?

First, realize that these things happen and you are not the first person faced with the problem. The main thing is exiting the zazen area as quickly and quietly as possible, then dealing with the problem in a manner and place where you can avoid disturbance to others if possible. If the problem is a serious medical emergency, though, you had better disturb at least one

person to summon aid!

"Quickly" does not mean carelessly or in a dash unless that is absolutely unavoidable. If possible, you should follow the normal sequence for exiting the zazen area—bowing as usual and walking sedately. The bows to your own side and the opposite side are perhaps more-than-usually appropriate in this case, forming your unseen apology to the others for creating a disturbance.

What happens after the problem event has been resolved, assuming that the event was not too serious, depends primarily on three elements: the customs of the group in which you are doing zazen, your confidence that you really are in good condition to finish the zazen period, and the approximate time remaining before the end of the period. If you left the zazen because of a coughing spell that you could not control, you probably can return to zazen when you are confident that there will be no more coughing. Realize, however, that zazen is an exceedingly quiet activity. If there are only ten minutes remaining until time for walking zazen or the end of zazen, it is better to wait until everyone starts moving. If there are forty minutes remaining, on the other hand, most groups will allow you to reenter quietly, bowing as usual and being as unobtrusive as possible.

Rules about leaving and reentering during a zazen period seldom are spelled out for newcomers. If you are lucky, you will have been aware of one or two others leaving the zazen at some time and of their return (or nonreturn) later. That provides some guidance. It is likely, though, that you can participate in zazen for several years without having such an experience. You then become an opportunity for others to learn about the group custom to allow or ban entrance during zazen by observing the leader's response to your entrance.

21. What should I do if I have to sneeze or cough?

Head colds are nearly as large a problem in a zazen group as in a concert hall. Ordinarily, much the same considerations apply. First, if possible don't take your cold to the zazen meeting. Colds are not an approved part of the compassionate sharing experience. Second, use a handkerchief, tissue, or even just your hand to stifle the noise and limit the area sprayed. Third, if it becomes clear that the coughing (or less commonly, the sneezing) is not going to end soon, quietly leave your cushion, preferably fluffing the cushion and bowing apologies to your neighbors and those opposite you just as you would at the end of the zazen period, and leave the room for a place where your problem will be less audible.

A related problem is the dripping nose. There probably is no faster, surer way to polarize a zazen group having both Japanese and Western participants than the arrival of a member with a running nose. Just letting one's nose drip, as was required by one U.S. group I heard of, seems unduly hard on the dripping person. Either of the two alternatives, however, is bound to set teeth on edge among either the Japanese or the Western contingent. Westerners tend to favor blowing the nose, albeit as quietly as possible. Most long-term Western zazen participants will confess to spending entire periods of zazen fighting the urge to go to a sniffling member, hand over some tissues, and firmly suggest blowing. The Japanese members, on the other hand, find public nose blowing a truly gross action. For that side, endless sniffling, regardless of noise level, is greatly preferable to blowing. Perhaps one might mentally tot up the relative numbers on hand and react in a way to offend the less-present culture.

22. After long periods of zazen, I notice I feel grouchy, and a friend reports the same thing. Is this a common occurrence?

It is probably not uncommon. I think the most likely cause is poor posture. When you sit motionless for a long period in an unbalanced posture, your body tenses to sustain the imbalance. A tense body leads to tense emotions. This is why posture is stressed so much: so your body and mind can be *un*stressed.

Another possible cause is an attachment to zazen itself. Particularly when you have been doing zazen alone for some time and then participate in group zazen, your mind is likely to follow up the sights and sounds of many people sitting together in a small area. Instead of sensing a sound and letting it go by, the greedy sitter thinks resentfully, "Who is that person disturbing *my* zazen?"

One time after doing only solitary zazen for a few months I was able to sit with a group of priests in a lovely temple deep in the mountains. Suddenly I realized with horror that I was perched on a zafu saying to myself, "You birds outside pipe down! It's time for *my* zazen, so no more chirping." With that realization, I finally began to do zazen.

WHAT IS A ZEN PRIEST?

1. Can I stay in your monastery?

There is a mistaken idea popular in Europe and the United States that Zen Buddhism is a monastic religion. It is not. If it were, and I had a monastery, quite probably you would be welcome to stay in it for awhile. Where I live, however, is a tiny apartment in a building adjacent to a temple. Even if you stayed in these cramped quarters, my daily routine and that of the resident priest and associate priest (scheduled to take over when the resident priest retires) are not at all what the word "monastery" brings to mind.

The basis of Japan's Zen priesthood is ministering to the temple members and other laypeople by sharing with them the Buddhist teachings and by providing them with the religious services of the sect. For those (few, in Japan) who wish to practice zazen, most Zen temples have zazen meetings. For those who wish to practice chanting sutras and to learn about the meaning of the sutras, most temples have sutra-reading and sutra-copying meetings. All temples perform the funerals and memorial services that are a central function of Japanese Buddhism.

Japan has no custom of outsiders, whether clergy or laity, staying in temples. The residential portion of a temple provides space for the resident priest, her/his family, and, perhaps, the priest who will become resident priest when the present one retires. There are no facilities in most

Zen temples for other people to stay. When funeral services are held in a temple, the bereaved family may spend the night between the Evening of Crossing service and the funeral itself remaining with the departed family member, but that means sleeping in a room normally used for meetings and with little provision for anything but sleeping and eating catered food. Even the bedding is often rented.

There are special training temples for new priests, but they seldom accept visitors. It is a difficult matter to prepare a new priest for a lifetime of service to laypeople during the brief term of one to five years that priest-trainees spend in such a temple. The time and attention of the head of the training temple, and those of any other teachers, are needed by the priest-trainees for whom they are responsible.

There are a few Zen temples, mostly in rural areas, that allow visitors to stay for awhile. In most cases, however, it is necessary to develop a relationship with the resident priest through attendance at weekly or monthly zazen meetings, sutra-reading meetings, and so forth, before a request for temporary residence will be accepted. In certain depopulated areas, some temples function as hostels to help maintain the temple. Those do not, however, have any practice program for the guests who come. They simply provide a place to sleep and, perhaps, some meals.

The only "Zen monastery" that I know of is not in Japan—it is in the United States, creating an institution that is now, and has been since the beginning, unknown in Japan.

2. Why do you say "clerics" or "priests" instead of "monks"?

Buddhism, unlike Catholicism, has no institution of monasticism and makes no distinction between those pursuing their own paths removed from society and those who serve laypeople. In Buddhism, it is expected that every cleric will devote great efforts toward full awakening as an individual in order to better assist others in awakening as well. In Buddhism, it is expected that every cleric will devote great care and understanding to meeting the religious needs of laypeople. A Buddhist cleric, unlike a Catholic one, can spend some periods of time withdrawn from ordinary society and other periods of time within ordinary society, serving the needs of that society. There is no need to choose one life or the other; Buddhist clerics normally, almost unanimously, live both lives. To view only one part of the Buddhist cleric's life as "religious" is to denigrate the

path of the bodhisattva, the path of pointing the way so that others may
join in walking it.

The institution of monasticism was developed in the early years of the Christian religion. The terms "monk" and "monastic" derive from a Greek word meaning "one, alone." As the *Encyclopedia of Religion* notes, "According to this etymology, therefore, the basic monastic person may be a hermit, a wandering ascetic, or simply someone who is not married or a member of a household. However, the term *monastic* normally refers to people living in community."

The original followers of Shakyamuni Buddha, who preceded Christianity by half a millennium, included four groups: male and female home leavers, and male and female householders. The home leavers were religious wanderers who relied on offerings for their food and clothing, traveling through most of the year and spreading the Buddhist teachings among householders along their paths. The home leavers thus suited the initial meaning of "monastics."

In Buddhism, as later in Christianity, what began as solitary hermits or wanderers evolved into fixed communities, often with extensive buildings and properties. The origins of Buddhist communities may be found in the custom of home leavers assembling during the three-month rainy season in India. This not only allowed shelter from the rains but also provided an opportunity for instruction of newer members and maintenance of the oral tradition of Buddhism's sacred texts. As the shelters became year-round communal dwellings, however, the character of the institution changed. For one thing, the communal centers became the locations for teaching and religious services for laypeople. Religious teaching and advice to laypeople had been a key role of the home leavers from the beginning of Buddhism. As the religion developed, religious services also became important. The "home leavers," who by then were leaving the "home" of their birth families only to enter another kind of "home" of their fellow religious leaders, became the specialists who performed those services on behalf of lay followers. In other words, they became priests.

The development of Mahayana Buddhism, including what became the Zen traditions, accentuated the departure from the concepts of monasticism. The defining characteristic of monasticism is, again quoting the *Encyclopedia of Religion*, that "monastic life, in contrast to the rest of human life, is entirely oriented toward a personal religious goal. . . . Monastic status is differentiated from other religious roles, offices, and functions in that it is not primarily based on performing some service to others in the religious tradition or to the larger society but on the more private cultivation of a path of transformation." Such private cultivation, pursued to the exclusion of service to laypeople, is directly opposed to the Mahayana ideal of the bodhisattva. A bodhisattva is one who is capable of buddhahood but delays entering the state of a buddha in order to assist others along the Buddhist path.

Even the more conservative Theravada Buddhism places great importance on providing teaching and services to laypeople, while stating that each individual must walk the Buddhist path individually.

Japanese Buddhism in general and the Zen sects in particular have long tended toward small, local temples with only one or two clerics. Those temples have existed precisely for the purpose of serving the laypeople of the local community. They exist today only with the continuing support of those laypeople. Clerics in local temples are accessible to their temple members and the community at large, whenever the need for their advice or service may arise.

Many people object to use of the word *priest,* saying that it means a person who stands between laypeople and their god(s). Certainly the Catholic use of priest has that meaning. It was precisely for this reason that Protestant Christian sects for the most part chose to use other terms, such as *minister* or *pastor.* My own preference, actually, would be to use *minister.* It derives from a word meaning servant, and its early uses signify serving the needs of others. Priest, on the other hand, comes from a word meaning elder. The widespread use of priest for religious professionals of almost any religion, however, and the specific history of its use in Western accounts of Japanese Buddhism, have established the term firmly.

The *Encyclopedia of Religion* notes two "identifying factors" of the core meaning of priest: "The priest, first, performs a sacrificial ritual, usually at a fixed location such as an altar. Second, the priest does so as a specialist on behalf of a community or congregation. When both of these factors are present, we have priesthood in a strict or narrow sense." Buddhist clerics of all branches and sects act in the ways specified, performing rituals in the center area of temples and dedicating both the act of chanting sutras and the offerings that have been made to the honor of the Buddha and other Buddhist beings or Buddhist people.

If Shakyamuni Buddha's followers had performed their wanderings without contact with laypeople, or without giving instruction to both householders and new home leavers, the teachings of the Buddha would have been lost in a single generation. If later Buddhist clerics had shut themselves within their centers and given no teaching, no advice, no religious services to laypeople, the centers and their clerics could not have endured. Whether we say priest or minister or (as some Western Buddhist groups have done) reverend, Buddhism has survived and spread, becoming a world religion, precisely because it has non-monastic clerics.

The terms *clergy* and *cleric* have accumulated less emotional baggage than have the other terms that might be used, so I often find it convenient to use these terms just to bypass the pervasive, unconscious but deeply felt (partly *because* it is unconscious) layers of connotation evoked by other terms.

3. What is the point in becoming a Zen cleric?

As has been widely noted in Zen books, the most common reason for Japanese (especially males) to enter the Zen priesthood is to succeed a parent as resident priest of the temple in which they were born. Those from non-temple families, and a number who are from temple families as well, choose to become priests for various reasons. The central point, however, is that they wish to serve the religious needs of laypeople.

Outside Japan, or for non-Japanese within Japan, the matter is a little different. Often there is no thought of serving in a temple or conducting religious observances apart from zazen. In my own case, it was a need to obtain training in acting as a zazen leader that prompted me to enter the clergy. By apprenticing to a Zen priest, I was able to participate in the training provided for new priests. During that training, however, I began to understand the reasons for religious practices other than just zazen. If both experience as a layperson and training as a new priest focus only on zazen, there is no opportunity for that vitally important lesson to be learned.

Some people, inside and outside Japan, want to become priests simply to obtain an easy means of support. Today's Japan, though, has few temples that can provide a reasonable livelihood to a priest who has no other source of income. That is why so many Zen priests have jobs outside their temples, sometimes in connection with their sects (as officers in head temples, training temples, or pilgrimage temples; as teachers in sect-sponsored schools and universities; in administrative jobs for the sect) or completely unconnected to religion (as civil servants, teachers, accountants, whatever).

A number of the Westerners I have met seem to have entered the priesthood primarily out of misunderstanding. Many of them first received the Buddhist precepts as householders (laypeople) then wanted to receive the precepts as home leavers (clerics). But those precepts are the same! The Zen sects rarely make any distinction between the precepts for the two groups. The precepts ceremony for laypeople is intended to provide for those who wish to follow the Buddhist path as individuals without assuming responsibility for the religious practice of others. It passes to the lay practitioner the precepts that were once received by the priest. This is performed in the expectation that formal acceptance of the precepts will help the practitioner in living in a Buddhist way. The same ceremony, performed as the first step in becoming a priest, is expected to be followed by formal training in a sect-certified training temple and by completion of the requirements for the ranks up to that qualifying the holder to act as a priest and to be appointed as the resident priest of a temple. For those who do not wish to become full priests, the precepts should be received as laypeople.

It has often puzzled me why anyone would wish to receive the precepts as a home leaver while having no wish or intention to do anything further in the clergy. The Zen sects deal with the results of this by removing the person's name from the register of the clergy after a certain time passes with no progress toward full standing as a priest. It is an unhappy reflection on the judgment of the priest to whom the dropout apprenticed when this happens.

Registration with the sect headquarters is the effective difference between receiving the precepts as a home leaver versus as a householder. Householders are registered only in the individual temple where they receive the precepts. Unfortunately several Zen priests, both Japanese and Western, have held precepts ceremonies for Westerners that they described as "home leaver" ceremonies without registering the recipients as new priest-trainees. That practice has caused considerable confusion among not only the recipients but also the other people in their Zen organizations.

The advantages of registration are that it is one prerequisite for enrollment in an authorized training temple and that changes of status are also recorded so that when the final standing as "ordained priest" is reached, there is a semipublic record of that fact. Although certification from a Zen sect as a person qualified to be resident priest of a temple does not mean anything with regard to a state of awakening, however that may be defined, it does show that the person involved has devoted quite a lot of time and effort to preparing for that position. The meaning of certification is much like that of a university degree: neither offers a guarantee of knowledge or deportment, but both do reflect a significant effort. If a priest wishes to be responsible for a temple that is formally affiliated with a Zen sect (that is, to be the resident priest of a temple registered in that sect), registration records must show that all requirements for that post have been met. Unrecorded training, or training at temples other than authorized training temples, is not accepted for certification regardless of the quality and rigor of that training. It thus behooves the priest-trainee, especially the Western priest-trainee, to inquire into sect requirements and whether they are being fulfilled.

4. How do you become an ordained cleric in Sōtōshū?

The first step, which is often the most challenging step for a non-Japanese or even for a Japanese who was not born in a temple family, is to find an ordained Sōtōshū cleric willing to accept you as an apprentice. A child born in a temple family, on the other hand, normally is apprenticed while still young to the parent who is a priest (this rarely means the mother).

Having been accepted in principle, the apprentice receives the sixteen Buddhist precepts used by Sōtōshū and a Buddhist name, along with a black buddha robe *(o-kesa),* black Chinese-style robe *(koromo),* and black miniature buddha robe *(rakusu)* from the master in a ceremony called *shukke tokudo,* "leaving home to benefit by the precepts."

My own shukke tokudo was performed on my forty-eighth birthday. Probably everyone is a bit nervous at taking this step, especially those who have not grown up in a temple, but I was excruciatingly nervous—right up until the ceremony itself, I did not know whether my head would be fully shaved as the first part of the ceremony. Having only one set of kimono and kimono underclothes, and not even a single set of priests' work clothes, I feared that I might have to complete my Japanese course in a Tokyo school while going about with a shaved head and normal Western clothes. What a relief when I learned that only one symbolic spot was to be shaved!

The apprentice usually also receives at this time the full set of gear needed by a priest-trainee. The items include eating bowls, utensils, and cloths; two boxes, one of woven bamboo and one lacquered, for travel, together with the cloths for carrying them; and the wide woven-bamboo hat, wrist-and-hand covers, ankle cloths, and straw sandals of the traveling trainee.

The master then submits to Sōtōshū administrative headquarters the required information about the new apprentice, including schooling, any work experience to date, and details of the shukke tokudo. Assuming all is in order, the apprentice is registered at headquarters as a Sōtōshū priest of the lowest rank, *jōza.* Jōza means ascending to the seat, the term used for starting zazen. A notice of registration is sent to the new apprentice from headquarters, via the master.

The next level is called *shuso.* This literally means the "head seat," designating the place in the priests hall that is reserved for the chief trainee during a three-month special practice period. An apprentice often serves as shuso in a temple other than that of the tokudo master. The temple may be a designated Sōtōshū training temple, which includes the two Sōtōshū head temples, in which there normally are two special practice periods each year, or may be a temple where a new resident priest is holding a special practice period as part of the installation procedures. Other temples may occasionally hold such practice with the approval of the administrative headquarters. In a training temple, the duties of the shuso are well defined and very active. In other temples, normally inhabited only by the resident priest, things are less clearly defined.

The main feature of the shuso's practice is performance of a ceremony formally called *risshin* (literally "standing the body") but more often spoken of as *hossenshiki,* the "dharma combat ceremony," because it involves a stylized debate between the shuso and several attending priests. This is a public ceremony, often attended by tens of priests and more than a hundred laypeople, especially when it is performed as part of the installation of a new resident priest. Confirmation of the completion of the shuso's term and ceremony is sent to Sōtōshū administrative headquarters. The shuso then is given the rank of *zagen* (literally "principal seat").

The next level, in contrast, is reached by a completely private ceremony, that of *dempō* (dharma transmission). Performed in a room sealed with special curtains, the dharma transmission is a ceremony attended only by the ordained priest who is transmitting the dharma and the apprentice who is receiving the dharma, possibly with the aid of two other ordained priests. The master from whom dharma transmission is received is called the apprentice's "true master." The relationship established at this time endures throughout the lifetime of the two participants. Permission must be obtained from administrative headquarters before dharma transmission can be performed, and the credentials of both master and apprentice are verified before permission is given. After the dharma transmission is completed, the master submits a statement to that effect and a request that the apprentice be permitted to perform the ceremony called *zuise* at the two head temples.

This step is also termed "changing color." The black buddha robe worn by a priest-trainee is now exchanged for the earth-colored, yellow-to-orange-to-brown, buddha robe of a full priest. The colored robe is worn for the first time at the head temple ceremonies. In these ceremonies, the "just-graduated" priest acts as officiating priest in an early morning service at each head temple (Eiheiji and Sōjiji). Upon completion of the ceremonies, the priest attains the rank of *oshō*.

The final step required for "ordination," which is to say for certification of competence to fulfill all duties of a Sōtōshū priest and to become the resident priest of a temple, is requesting certification as a *kyōshi* (literally "religious teacher"). This certification can be granted only if the requesting priest not only has completed the progression from jōza to oshō but also has completed the necessary period as a student in an official Sōtōshū training temple. The average training period is two years; some priests may stay longer and some, shorter periods. The training temple period for someone who has completed a bachelor's degree from an accredited university (in Japan or anywhere else) can be shorter than that for persons having less academic education. A priest wishing to be resident priest of a high-ranked temple, or to be the head of a training temple someday, may spend several additional years in a training temple. A priest who must suddenly take over a temple as a result of the unexpected death of the resident priest may be granted certification despite a shorter period in a training temple.

The series of initial ranks rely on the training given by, and evaluations made by, only one or two individual priests. The training temple has a special value, in addition to its role as a seminary, in that it exposes the priest-trainee to the teachings and methods of several priests and shows the priest-trainee's capabilities and character to several priests. This broadens the trainee's outlook and understanding while providing an outside verification of the trainee.

The training temple period can be performed at any time after the trainee has entered the priesthood as a jōza. In most cases, it is completed before the occurrence of dharma transmission. In any event, though, it must be completed before the priest becomes a "religious teacher," certified by Sōtōshū to perform all religious services of the sect and to become resident priest of a Sōtōshū temple.

Writers in Western languages often wrongly use the word "ordination" as a translation of the initial ceremony through which a layperson enters the priesthood and starts training. Instead, Sōtōshū "ordination" really does not occur until the administrative headquarters issues the certificate of a "religious teacher." So after all the traditional ceremonies with their weight of historic and emotional meaning, "ordination" itself is a matter of the simple receipt of a piece of paper.

5. How do you become an ordained cleric in Rinzaishū or Ōbakushū?

There are fewer ceremonies and more levels in Rinzaishū and Ōbakushū than in Sōtōshū, but the general pattern is very similar. Here, for example, we will discuss the Myōshinji Rinzaishū pattern.

The first step, as in Sōtōshū, is the ceremony of receiving the Buddhist precepts and entering the priesthood as a trainee. The starting rank is called *shami,* a term that derives from the Sanskrit term for one who has just entered the Buddhist path. One can become a shami at the age of five. The next three ranks are attained by application to the head temple (in this example, Myōshinji), showing that one has reached the required age, general education level, and experience of Zen practice. The fifth rank, called *zendo,* requires that a holder of the fourth rank passes a written test, writes an acceptable thesis on a Buddhist topic, and completes at least one year of formal training in a head temple priests hall (training temple). For the Myōshinji sect, training can be performed at Myōshinji itself or at any of four other head temples of Rinzai sects (Kenchōji, Engakuji, Daitokuji, and Tōfukuji). Upon attaining the rank of zendo, the priest performs a ceremony comparable to the Sōtōshū zuise. The priest then can be said to be "ordained" and can become the resident priest of a Myōshinji Rinzaishū temple. The honorific *zenji* is used for Rinzaishū priests of this rank or higher. There are nine ranks above that of zendo, the highest of which is that held only by the kanchō (chief priest of the sect).

Shaving one's head upon entering a religious life is an ancient and wide-spread custom. In Buddhism, it symbolizes cutting off attachments to things of this world of illusion. The ending of such attachments is one of the main teachings of Buddhism, so it is not surprising that the custom of head shaving has endured.

One result of shaving the heads of clerics is the easy recognition of clerical status. This both identifies the depilated head's body as someone presumed to deserve a certain amount of respect and reminds the bearer of the depilated head of the need to earn that respect, not just for oneself but for all clerics. The latter effect may engender a degree of propriety in public actions of clerics, certainly a salutary result.

The first movement away from head shaving came with Jōdo Shinshū. In line with that sect's teachings concerning the Age of the Decay of the Dharma, in which clerics are no more capable than laypeople of following the Buddhist path through their own efforts, the government early gave permission for Jōdo Shinshū clerics to marry, eat meat, and appear in public with unshaved heads and nonclerical clothing. The use of everyday clothing and omission of head shaving made Jōdo Shinshū priests visually indistinguishable from their temple members.

Following the Meiji Restoration of 1868, government regulations concerning Buddhism were repealed one after another. The new government sought to weaken the influence of Buddhism, still viewed as a foreign religion after nearly 1,300 years. Japan's indigenous religious practices were, instead, developed into an organized religion called Shinto. That religion was officially promoted in an effort to heighten national consciousness among the Japanese people. Changes at that time included the repeal of the laws requiring non–Jōdo Shinshū clerics to shave their heads and to wear only distinctively Buddhist clothing in public. The new laws did not, however, go so far as to forbid head shaving.

The result is that today most, but not nearly all, Buddhist clerics keep their heads shaved. The Zen sects, as conservative, established religions, encourage shaved heads among the clergy. Except in training temples for new priests, however, they do not require shaving.

Women seem less likely than men to let their hair grow in at times. I have known two women Sōtōshū clerics, though, who let their hair grow.

One was a young woman still living in Tokyo as a research fellow and rarely active in her role as priest. The other was the middle-aged resident priest of a rural temple with a nursery school attached to it, who was also the caregiver for an elderly, disabled priest retired from a women's training temple. With a day that included not just chanting sutras but also driving a school bus and administering a large school, she apparently found short hair and Western-style clothing (of a conservative design) more practical than a shaved head and clerical wear.

7. What is the meaning of the clothing worn by Zen priests?

The history of Buddhism, with its transmission from India to Japan, is recorded in the clothing of Japan's Buddhist priests. The outermost garment is the buddha robe (o-kesa), a rectangle of cloth that is tied over the left shoulder leaving the right shoulder uncovered, just as the one worn by Shakyamuni Buddha and still worn by Buddhist clerics in India and Southeast Asia. Sometimes instead of the full buddha robe, however, a smaller rectangle is worn suspended by a strap around the neck (rakusu). Beneath the buddha robe is a Chinese-style over-robe with long, very deep sleeves (koromo). Finally, beneath the over-robe is a Japanese kimono. (For myself and, I suppose, most Western Buddhist clerics, the further movement Westward is symbolized by Western-style underclothes beneath the Japanese kimono underclothes.)

In the Zen sects, a black buddha robe signifies that the wearer is a priest-trainee. The black buddha robe is worn over a black or navy blue over-robe, and either a white kimono or a kimono in a solid, subdued color such as gray. White is viewed as special, so the white kimono is used mostly for special ceremonies and for services for the temple members.

The most often encountered set of robes is a white or subdued-colored kimono, a black over-robe, and a buddha robe that is in the color range between yellow, orange, and brown. It is said that when Shakyamuni Buddha left home and became a wandering ascetic he used earth to dye scraps of white shroud cloth for his clothing. Thus we still wear buddha robes in the tones that might be produced by mud dyes. These are the robes of a qualified priest.

For special ceremonies and for the funerals and memorial services conducted for temple members, however, the officiating priest often wears a colored over-robe and a buddha robe of another color and perhaps made of brocade or having embroidery. By wearing the most formal, most expensive clothes, the officiating priest honors the temple member who has died. In these cases, the priest may also wear a hat that has long rectangular panels down the back of the head and back of the shoulders.

The over-robe, with its sleeves that are both deep and wide, is often mistaken for a cowled cloak. I was greatly puzzled when a friend asked me something about my "robe with a cowl." It was some time afterward that the same friend saw me tie cords in the sleeves of my over-robe so as to gather the sleeves at my shoulders, then secure the lower portions of the sleeves to my body with a cord around my waist. The gathered sleeves were what she had taken for a cowl. Because the sleeves are so large, they need to be fastened out of the way when one is placing objects on the altar and removing them from the altar, or for any task in which swaying cloth might pose a hazard.

The traditional costume of a priest-trainee traveling about to seek training and experience is a kimono and black over-robe, both tucked around the hips to free the lower legs, with a black miniature buddha robe, woven straw hat, white cloths covering the backs of the hands, white cloths around the ankles, and straw sandals. Two small cases may be hung over the shoulders so that one is on the chest and the other on the back. These carry the clerical trainee's essentials. The buddha robe, sutra books, and other such items are in the front, lacquered, box, which is enclosed in a cloth case on which the eating bowls and implements are secured. Shaving gear, soap, and a white kimono are in the woven straw case on the back. This same costume is used for the religious practice called *takuhatsu*, in which one priest or (more properly) a group of priests walk through an area chanting sutras and inviting residents to offer food (or nowadays, money). For takuhatsu, though, the cases over the shoulders are omitted and the main eating bowl is held in the hands to receive donations. At rice harvest time, a long tube of cloth may be hung around the shoulders, with both ends tied; rice offerings are accumulated in the cloth.

For going outside the temple, and for such events as meetings with other priests or with laypeople inside the temple, a white or colored kimono may be worn with a modified over-robe having sleeves the same size as those of the kimono and having fewer pleats in the bottom half. A miniature buddha robe, not the full-size buddha robe, is worn with this modified over-robe.

Work and errands, whether inside or outside the temple grounds, usually call for traditional Japanese work clothes, called samu-e or samu-gi. The pants are full cut, gathered at waist and ankles with cords or, nowadays, elastic. The top portion is cut like a kimono but fastens with ties instead of being held in place with separate cords. The ordinary top portion reaches only to the hips, but a somewhat-more-formal version has a top falling below the knees. Clerical work clothes are always without pattern and are usually of a subdued color—black for trainees (or for very modest, traditional full priests), and dark blue, brown, and gray are typical. Recently, though, samu-e have become fashionable. Makers of traditional Japanese craft objects probably were the inspiration for the fashion; they often find samu-e both suitable and comfortable. Those who took up the style simply for fashion's sake have created a vogue for patterned cloth, sometimes in bright colors.

8. What is a typical day in the life of a priest?

My routine when I was Taisōji's sole assistant priest is not too unlike that of a resident priest in a small, rural temple. Although temple-related matters more than fill the time of a resident priest in a large, urban temple, such matters are concentrated in early morning, evening, and weekends for priests with fewer temple members.

Morning started at 5:25 every day, year round; the only exceptions were the two or three annual sesshin, when the day started at 4:30. By 5:45, I was dressed in kimono and black over-robe, with the clothing beneath the kimono varying according to the season. In those days, Taisōji had no heating or cooling in the main hall, so thermal long johns were an essential part of my winter outfit. So was a thick vest lined with curly wool, worn between the kimono and over-robe. Before 6:00, I had walked around the corner to the temple, entered the main hall, and opened all the wooden shutters. Japanese shutters are not hinged like Western shutters. Instead they are sliding panels that stack within a single-width enclosure on the outer wall. The stacking is a manual affair. My morning exercise consisted of pushing a bulky shutter, taller than myself, along its track, reaching as far across the enclosure as I could to push the shutter outward against the wall of the enclosure, then repeating the process for each of the remaining five shutters in turn. There are only two walls of six shutters each, so I was thankful when I reached the windows, with a mere two shutters each and not nearly as tall as those on the glass doors.

While I was opening up, the resident priest entered the main hall unless he had to be away from Tokyo for the morning. Starting promptly at 6:00, we performed the morning sutra chanting. In Sōtōshū's two head temples, and in training temples as well, morning sutra chanting often occupies ninety minutes or more. Fortunately for me, and my arthritic knees, Taisōji's sutras require only about fifteen minutes. On the four mornings each week that we held zazen, the sutra chanting was delayed until the end of zazen so that the laypeople participating in zazen could also participate in the sutra chanting.

After opening and sutras, or after just opening the hall, I returned home for breakfast. On zazen days, that meant preparing and eating something quickly enough to be back at the temple in the zazen hall by 7:00, so it would be open and ready to receive participants for the 7:30 zazen session. At 8:10, we concluded zazen and moved to the main hall for morning sutras, finishing at 8:30. Most Japanese offices start work at 9:00, and stores do not open until 10:00, so this schedule allowed the lay participants to reach their work on time.

When morning sutra chanting was finished, I was finished with daily temple duties until the end of the afternoon. At 5:00 in winter or 6:00 in summer, I returned to the main hall to remove the day's food and tea offerings from the altars, slide all the shutters back out of their cabinets, and close the hall.

Most of the memorial services were (and are) held on weekends. The gradual entry of Japan into a five-day work week was clearly evidenced in the slow shift from having nearly all memorial services on Sundays to having them divided between Saturdays and Sundays in increasingly even proportions. I did the main temple cleaning on Sunday morning at first, immediately after breakfast so as to be ready for the first service at 9:30 or 10:00. Over the years, that shifted to doing the main cleaning on Saturday morning, with just a quick pass with vacuum cleaner and duster on Sunday morning. Changing clothes from kimono and over-robe to work clothes, then back again, made me feel like a fashion model doing a speed change! Whether on one day or two, there always seemed to be enough services to occupy the resident priest and me until 2:00 or 3:00 in the afternoon. The pause for lunch was less than thirty minutes, so I learned to slurp noodles in soup at almost Japanese speed.

The period from the end of one memorial service to the start of the next was my busiest interval. Before the start of a service, there were offerings of flowers, fruit, or sweets to be properly arranged on the altar. Flower arrangement was simple because the florists tied the flowers in beautifully arranged bunches, so all that was needed was to place them in vases. Some days there were so many flowers that those from an early service had to be moved to a bucket so the same vase could be used for a later service. Fruit arranging was another matter. I had never realized, before taking up temple life at Taisōji, that fruit arranging is also an art. Occasionally someone brought a basket filled with carefully arranged fruit. Most of the time, though, I had to stack varying numbers of different fruits on top of two footed trays with no edges to hold the fruits on the trays. Asian pears, which are quite hard, had to be placed below, for example, snow peaches. Grapefruit, which are large, should normally be at the bottom of the pyramid, but what to do when there are also apples as large as the grapefruit and much heavier? Grapes and bananas always go on top, with occasional puzzles about which to give precedence in non-squashable positions. Then, with the altar all decorated and candles and incense ready, there were the *o-tōba,* memorial markers, to stand in racks in front of the altar. (For a description of memorial markers, see "What are the main Buddhist holidays marked by temples?") Had there been only one priest in the temple, which is the most common case, the same priest would have to greet the members arriving for memorial services, quickly write more markers when someone had neglected to request them in advance, answer telephone calls about upcoming memorial service schedules, and generally perform sixteen other tasks simultaneously.

Watching, and occasionally giving active direction to, the guests entering the hall for each service was a source of much revelation and not infrequent astonishment about the social habits of the Japanese. After the leading relative (and spouse) entered and sat halfway down the front row, making that row as far back toward the sliding doors as possible, three people or so sat in the second row and everyone else tried to sit in the back row. Of course by that time there was not really enough space in front of the sliding doors to make a third row anyway, so they opened the sliding doors and sat in the storage area behind the door slides. If I had not already firmly herded everyone into one side of the room, and especially if there were enough people that both sides would be fully occupied, this went on more or less simultaneously on the left and right, enlivened by brisk changes of side at intervals. In winter, when there were heated carpets for the guests to sit on, it was a foregone conclusion that all middle-aged men would be seated on carpets, sometimes even allowing their wives to sit beside them, and all the women over seventy would be back on the uncarpeted area, directly on tatami, where the wind would blow across their feet and knees throughout the service. At other times of year, they managed to seat themselves directly in the path that must be taken by the resident priest to enter and leave the main hall. Purses, coats, and shopping bags, of course, were piled in the corridor that must be used by attendees as well as by the resident priest. Provided I spotted that maneuver in time, I cleared the entire collection out of the corridor and into an area adjacent to the entry-exit path, hoping to indicate that as a non-sitting zone. The entire sequence required at least ten minutes if there were more than about ten attendees, so services grew progressively behind schedule as the day went along.

Weekend services generally were finished about in time for the telephone to start ringing. My telephone rate was only a tiny fraction of that of the resident priest, because I generally had phone conversations only with the Westerners associated with Taisōji. With luck, I might get through the calls coming in before it was time to close up the temple.

On weekdays, if there were no memorial services or funerals, I could work at home doing copyediting of English translations prepared by Japanese translators. Mostly the subject area was electrical or electronics. The resident priest of a small temple would spend that time in temple maintenance (including maintenance of the grounds, a never-ending chore especially in autumn when the leaves are falling). Then there are preparations to be made for the weekend's memorial services. If there is to be a funeral, the regular altar must be curtained off or rearranged so that a special funeral altar can be set up. Other priests must be summoned to help with the services (see "What is a Zen funeral like?"), a suitable precepts name must be devised, and the words to pull the deceased to the "other shore" of death (from "this shore" of life) must be written.

Other temple activities are held on weekdays (such as sutra-reading group, women's group, senior citizens' group). If the priest gives lessons in traditional arts, the lessons are scheduled for weekdays as much as possible. And of course if the priest must hold an outside job, that job is performed on weekdays.

Temple life is a busy life, filled not with zazen and composition of haiku poems, as Western visitors seem to assume, but with a continuous stream of chores that must be done, people who must be talked with, and lastly, religious services that must be conducted, including zazen.

9. What is a typical day in the life of a priest-trainee?

The daily schedule in a training temple is almost as variable as that in a normal neighborhood temple. It depends on the activities that are necessary on a particular day, on the department a trainee is assigned to, and on the characteristics of the individual training temple, among other factors.

My own schedule in the Toyama training temple for women changed often and was, in any case, regulated by bells and drums, not clocks. So I was seldom aware of the clock time and cannot tell you what might constitute a typical day. I spent a great deal of time at another temple dedicated to Zen practice and without any lay members requiring memorial services, but the schedule there was an attempt at re-creating the schedule described by Dōgen. A more typical pattern, then, is that once published by a training temple for women:

4:00	Wake up
4:15–5:00	Zazen
5:00–6:15	Morning sutra chanting
6:15–7:45	Cleaning
7:45–8:15	Morning meal
8:15–9:30	Individual study time
9:30–12:00	Class (sewing buddha robes, sewing kimono, lecture on a Zen text, flower arranging, chanting practice, or calligraphy)
12:00–12:30	Midday (main) meal
12:30–13:30	Free time
13:30–15:00	Work period
15:00–15:30	Tea
15:30–16:00	Free time
16:00–16:30	Evening sutra chanting
16:30–17:30	Individual study time

17:30–18:00	Evening meal	
18:00–20:15	Cleaning, bath	
20:15–21:00	Zazen	
21:00	Lights out	

Things rarely work out this tidily, however. There are days when laypeople come to the temple for a zazen meeting, special service, or lecture, for example; on those days, "free time" and individual study times are cancelled in favor of preparations, participation, and cleanup afterward. Teachers have their own temples and their own special schedules, so a class may be postponed or may be extended through a longer period according to the teacher's availability. The classes, by the way, are the same in training temples for men and for women. Classes cover the skills needed by a priest, regardless of sex.

10. Are there any women Zen priests?

Yes indeed, there are women clergy in nearly all of Japan's sects, including the Zen sects. The 1995 Japanese government survey of religious organizations showed that approximately 37 percent of the Buddhist clergy consisted of women. The actual value is somewhat higher even, because one sect that has a very large number of clerics, a wide majority of whom are women, no longer maintains records of how many clerics are male and how many are female.

The level of female participation in the Zen sect clergy, however, is quite low. The same survey shows a total of 23,205 Zen clerics, 1,484 of whom are women, making us only about 6 percent of the total. My own sect, Sōtōshū, is even lower, at about 5 percent.

The status of women in the clergy has varied widely in Japanese history, together with the general status of women in society. It appears that the historic low point for women's standing in Japan's Buddhist clergy occurred in 1941. The absence of male clerics during World War II forced a relaxation of restrictions that had been imposed during the 1930s, and postwar trends continued the improvement.

Few Japanese today realize that the first three Buddhist priests who were born on Japanese soil were all young women, daughters of families that had come from China or Korea, bringing both Buddhism and the full scope of continental culture with them. One of the key aspects of that culture was written language, which had not previously existed in Japan. Before literacy spread, it was only the immigrant families that could read the Buddhist scriptures.

The three, led by one who received the Buddhist name Zenshinni, received the initial precepts in 584 from a Korean priest who had immigrated to Japan. After early hardships related to disputes about the acceptance of Buddhism in Japan, the three women, still in their teens, were allowed to go to the Korean peninsula for training. There they received the full precepts and became *bhikkhunis,* female priests. Upon their return to Japan, the three transmitted the precepts to Japan's first native-born *bhikkhus,* male priests, and to another group of native-born bhikkhunis.

Early Japanese history also records that in 741 the imperial court ordered construction of two temples in each of Japan's provinces, one for male and one for female priests. Those for female priests were specifically required to have women as the chief priests.

Dōgen, founder of Japan's Sōtō sect, wrote high praise for a woman priest in his recorded sayings and correspondence as well as in one chapter in particular of his *Shōbōgenzō* (Eye Treasury of the Right Dharma). The chapter titled "Raihai-tokuzui" (Bowing in Reverence and Realizing the Essence) originated as a lecture at Kōshōji, the first Sōtōshū temple, in Kyoto, given in early March 1240. Even the abridged version that is used in most editions of the *Shōbōgenzō* gives prominence to two female Chinese Zen masters, Mo-shan, a contemporary of Rinzai, and Miao-hsin. The complete version of this chapter incorporates considerably more praise for the Buddhist understanding of various women priests. Dōgen also refers in his recorded sayings to at least three women to whom he gave teachings, one of whom is identified as his own apprentice. The exact standings and later accomplishments of these women, however, are not known.

In Rinzaishū, there is Mugai Nyodai, the first woman in Japan definitely known to have been fully qualified as a Zen priest. Before her death in 1298, she founded a series of temples called the Five Mountains Women's Temples, paralleling the Five Mountains Zen Temples for men. This group expanded during her lifetime to include fifteen temples in the Kyoto area. A generation later, it had grown much larger in Kyoto and had spread to five temples in Kamakura as well.

Despite later restrictions imposed on women in all of Japan's Buddhist sects, the differences between male and female clerics have always been

differences of degree, not of kind. Women always were able to officiate at $\quad$
the Buddhist rites conducted on behalf of laypeople. So yes, there definitely are now, and have always been women Zen priests.

11. Why can male priests marry but female priests cannot?

The ban against female priests marrying is a total fiction originating in the minds of people who have never bothered to check the regulations they cite. Sōtōshū is typical in its solution to the problems associated with married priests: there is not one line in one Sōtōshū regulation that says anything about priests marrying, whether they be male, female, or hermaphrodite.

The entire matter of married priests has a long history in Japan.

When Buddhism entered Japan from Korea and China, Buddhist clerics were required to maintain celibacy. We are often told (incorrectly) that the status of marriage and the clergy remained the same until 1872, when the new government under the Meiji emperor passed a law stating that "from now on Buddhist clerics shall be free to eat meat, marry, grow their hair, and so on. Furthermore, there will be no penalty if they wear ordinary clothing when not engaged in religious activities." If challenged on the point, a Japanese informant might recall that the government had permitted marriage (and meat and hair) to clerics of the Jōdo Shinshū and Shugendō sects of Buddhism for several hundred years. The heart of the matter lay not in Buddhist scriptures and their interpretation but rather in Japanese government regulations. Government control of religion was inherited by Japan from China at the same time that Buddhism was inherited.

From the early seventeenth century until the Meiji Restoration in 1868, the Tokugawa shoguns attempted to restore seventh-century codes governing religion and the clergy. Results, predictably, were uneven. Even before that time, the pattern of clerical marriage and temple inheritance had long been established in Japan. There are indications of family successions in the priesthood as early as the Heian period, from 794 to 1185. Legal rights of a (male) cleric's children (read "sons") to inherit the cleric's property were formally recognized during that period. By 914, the imperial court complained that two-thirds of the people claimed to be clerics and most of them had families and amassed heritable (and nontaxable) property. References to married clerics exist through the succeeding periods, right up to the 1872 change in the law.

The more-formally recognized exceptions to the celibacy requirement were the Jōdo Shin sect founded by Shinran Shōnin and the Shugendō sects that integrated Buddhism, Shinto, and early Japanese folk religion focusing on mountain austerities. Shinran was an advocate of the theory that by his times, in the thirteenth century, the Buddhist "Age of the Decay of the Dharma" had been reached. With true Buddhist teachings no longer available, went the theory, there was no choice but to rely on the vow of Amida Buddha to bring all beings to awakening. That being the case, said Shinran, there was no reason to distinguish between clerical and lay status in such matters as diet, appearance, and marriage.

It is now widely accepted among Zen and other Buddhist scholars in Japan that the primary effect of the 1872 law was to provide a measure of legality, and thus of security, to the wives and children who certainly existed in great numbers.

For the most part, today's Japanese temple members prefer a married priest for much the same reasons usually cited in Protestant Christianity: stability, the availability of added persons to care for the temple, and the priest's understanding of the difficulties encountered by married temple members.

12. How are priests appointed to temples?

It probably will come as a disappointment to those who have visions of dharma combats to determine who has the right to a temple, but the real-life process is extremely prosaic. In most cases, the priest who becomes the new resident priest of a temple is the senior (probably the only) apprentice of the former resident priest. Given that most Zen temples have male resident priests and that most of those male priests are married, the position of resident priest is often said to be inherited. This is not literally true, but it does suggest a very common process of succession from father to son. Nowadays, we sometimes see succession from father to daughter or from mother to daughter or son. A resident priest whose children do not consent to enter the priesthood will often seek to marry a daughter to a priest who is not already designated as the heir to another temple. When all these family processes fail, a new resident priest is sought from the outside, normally by referral through priesthood friends.

In any case, the new resident priest must be formally approved by the temple's board of directors, which sends the sect headquarters a request for the appointment to be made. The chief priest of the sect then issues a certificate of appointment. An installation ceremony may be held after that certificate has been issued.

A resident priest looking forward to retirement may decide to appoint a "successor apparent." The Japanese term for this position is *fukujūshoku.* The *jūshoku* portion means resident priest, and the *fuku* prefix signifies one level downward. It may be translated as associate priest. One friend of mine made bilingual professional cards when she was appointed by her father as fukujūshoku. The English side showed her position as "vice priest"! I suggested that some other term might be more suitable, and we eventually settled on "associate priest." Another Japanese term for assistant implies a permanent relationship as subordinate rather than one as successor, so it seemed better to avoid assistant as well as vice. (For example, I am an assistant priest; one of the resident priest's apprentices is now the associate priest, and two of his other apprentices are assistant priests.) If the resident priest retires, dies, or becomes disabled, the associate priest can immediately take over the duties as resident priest.

13. Why is it usual for priests' sons to inherit temples?

The custom of a son succeeding his father as resident priest of a temple was already ancient when the Meiji Restoration led to legalization of marriage for Zen priests. Many religions have discovered that enforcing non-marriage is a task much more likely of accomplishment than is enforcing celibacy. So "celibate" priesthoods have often produced sons to follow in those priesthoods. Japanese Buddhism's traditions of apprenticeship have also, almost from the beginning, resulted in the effective adoption of children into the priesthood. Originally (as in Catholicism) children were often presented to a temple to be educated as priests from their earliest years. That custom still endures, though to a lesser degree. One of Japan's leading Zen priests has often remarked about how she was given at the age of five to an aunt who raised her in a temple.

One of the characteristics of Buddhism is that the priests live within the temple grounds. In Japan, the resident priest's living quarters normally are within the same building as the main hall or are connected to that hall by an enclosed passage. The only home known by most priests during childhood and adulthood, whether they enter that temple by birth or by early adoption, is the temple home. It is natural, then, that when a priest retires there is a wish to remain in the temple that has always been "home." The same is true of an aging, perhaps widowed, spouse of a priest. If a priest from outside the family becomes the new resident priest, however, that priest cannot be expected to take over the care of one or more aging non-relations. One important reason for wishing to be succeeded by one's child is just that simple.

People in all walks of life who have lived happily and in fulfillment through their occupations will always, I think, hope that their children will follow the same occupation. In that way, we may hope that our children will find the happiness and fulfillment that have blessed our own lives.

Now that most Japanese priests are married, the temple members are likely to prefer that the temple remain in the hands of a single family. Children of the resident priest grow up in the midst of temple life, surrounded by the children of temple members. Associations formed around the temple in childhood thus can continue through adulthood.

Before the Meiji Restoration, temples were more or less rigorously classified as those having male resident priests and those having female resident priests. Now, however, the classifications are formally abandoned (and slowly melting away in practice). It is no longer uncommon for a daughter to succeed her father or a son, his mother. The natural wish for an enduring family home remains the same.

14. Why do some priests have jobs apart from their temples?

Japan's shift from a rural, agricultural society to an urban, industrialized society has, among many other results, left many Buddhist temples without sufficient membership to support the temple upkeep, let alone a priest and priest's family. The method of bridging the gap between income and outgo in the clergy is much the same as elsewhere: additional paid work.

Just as many Western churches and all (I believe) Western Zen centers are individual entities, legally separate from each other, Japan's Buddhist temples are almost all individual "religious corporations." The various Buddhist sects, including Sōtōshū, Rinzaishū, and Ōbakushū, are called "umbrella religious corporations." Funds flow from the individual religious corporations (meaning local temples) to the umbrella religious corporation with which they choose to affiliate. The umbrella corporation provides services to the local temples, such as maintaining registers of temples and priests, supporting the formal training of new priests, and

publishing materials related to the sect. Responsibility for the affairs of
each temple (each religious corporation), however, rests with the board of
directors of that temple. The resident priest normally chairs the board of
directors. In effect, this means that the priest is responsible for maintenance of the temple and its activities.

Some priests can supplement the income at their own temples with
income from other temples, whether those others are popular places to
visit or are training temples (or both). Another possibility is giving
instruction in Japanese traditional arts, such as tea ceremony, flower
arranging, calligraphy—or in English conversation. Some temples have
affiliated schools, mostly at the preschool and kindergarten level. Even
these activities, however, often fail to cover the shortfall. Rather than
attempting to obtain overly large amounts from the temple members,
most priests then try to obtain outside work that leaves weekends and
evenings free for temple duties. It is a difficult life, but certainly a better
solution than closing the temple and letting it fall into ruin. I rather sus-
pect that the recent tentative acceptance of daughters as successors to their
resident-priest fathers may have something to do with allowing a son-in-
law to continue a career that supports the family and the temple. Certainly
outside work by the resident priest's spouse is a frequent source of necessary income for a temple family.

A 1995 survey by one Zen sect showed that only 17 percent of surveyed
temples had memberships greater than the 200 families considered a
minimum to support a temple. Total temple income for the previous year
was less than 1 million yen (U.S. $9,785) in 29 percent of reporting tem-
ples and less than 3 million yen (U.S. $29,000) in another 25 percent. Bear
in mind that this income must cover building repairs and such emergen-
cies as a retaining wall for a cemetery washed out by torrential rains, in
addition to regular expenses and living costs of the priest and family members. Only 1.5 percent of responding temples reported that temple income
covered all temple expenses, whereas 24 percent of temples had income
covering less than half their expenses. No wonder, then, that both resident
priests and their spouses often hold outside jobs unrelated to the temple.

15. Can I become a Zen priest without going to Japan?

For the most part, the answer at this time is no. There are various movements within the United States to establish uniform training requirements

and registration for Zen priests, but these are not yet at the functional stage. Sōtōshū has established two special ranks of the priesthood for those who both train and serve outside Japan. Some of the persons in that category have had varying amounts of formal training in Japan but without fulfilling all the requirements for normal certification ("ordination"). Others have never trained in Japan.

The duties and circumstances of priests in Western Zen centers have little in common with those of priests in Japanese temples. For this reason, a separate training regime and certification system would probably prove advantageous. Meanwhile many—probably most—Western Zen leaders either have no formal training and registration or have training and registration that are recognized only by their own group and closely affiliated groups.

The training temples for Japan's Zen sects lack experience, resources, and a sense of need for establishing separate training regimes designed for priest-trainees for other nations, having quite enough difficulty in managing the programs for those who will serve in Japan's temples. Despite this, and in the face of severe language and cultural problems, a number of non-Japanese priest-trainees have entered the regular training programs of Japan's Zen sects, and many of them have persevered to graduation. Most then return to their home countries to lead Zen centers, rather than Japanese-style temples, but a few (myself included) have remained in Japan and function as "Japanese" priests. It obviously is possible, then, to train and qualify in Japan. This is another factor in the lack of Japanese concern for overseas training facilities.

16. Why is there such a distinction between priests and laypeople?

At a fundamental level, Buddhism makes no distinction between clergy and laity. The original Buddhist *sangha,* those who followed the teachings of Shakyamuni Buddha, included the four categories of female and male home leavers, and female and male householders. These led to today's clergy and laity. The role of the Buddhist clergy is a support role, of teaching, presenting a model of Buddhist life, and preserving knowledge of sacred texts and rites. A sutra chanting by a layperson is no less respectful to the memorialized dead or appreciated buddhas than is the same chanting by a priest.

Complaints about discrimination between priests and laypeople usually arise when Westerners engage in forms of Buddhist practice that are normally felt, in Asia, to be needed only by priests and priest-trainees. In some branches of Buddhism, those who want to engage in concentrated Buddhist practice for a period of time are made into something resembling temporary clerics. These temporary clerics then are treated in the same manner as any other clerics of similar (low) rank. Japanese Buddhism, however, has not followed that custom.

When a Zen temple in Japan requires a large number of priests, for an occasion such as the annual summer general memorial services or the installation of a new resident priest, the priests of other temples in that sect fill the required roles. In many parts of Japan, a normal funeral service is performed by at least five priests and often more; the priests of the same sect in each area all cooperate to assist each other in these services.

When an American Zen center encounters a need for more than one or two priests, the usual solution is to assign laypeople to the remaining positions. There is nothing wrong with this; it simply is not necessary, and thus not customary, in Japan.

Both clergy and laypeople in Japan assume, almost unanimously, that there are roles for priests and other roles for laypeople, and that those roles are best kept separate. During most of Japan's Buddhist history, government regulations specified the licensing of those clerics deemed capable of instructing laypeople in Buddhist teachings, as well as those deemed capable of maintaining temples as resident priests. Even the new religions that emphasize active involvement of laypeople generally have a system of limiting leadership roles to those who have completed some form of education in the sect.

I understand that some Christian churches in the Americas and Europe now share their pulpits with laypeople on certain occasions. Even in such cases, though, it is clear that the layperson involved is not considered a cleric and is not expected to have the education and specialized knowledge of a cleric.

The question from the Western side is "Why can't laypeople do thus-and-so?" (for example, give a lecture during a zazen meeting). From the Japanese side, it is "Why would a layperson want to do that, and why would the clerics and other laypeople present want a layperson to do it?"

WHAT ARE ZEN
RELIGIOUS SERVICES LIKE?

1. What activities are there in Zen temples besides zazen?

The most-frequent activity in any of Japan's Buddhist temples is the memorial service. There are also funerals and special temple services. Of the activities that involve laypeople in more than a passive spectator role, most Zen temples conduct sutra-reading sessions, sutra-copying sessions, and Buddhist music practice. The temple also may sponsor youth activities and clubs, clubs for senior citizens, clubs for young adults and middle-aged adults, clubs for sports or games (such as Japanese chess), and community activity groups. Before 1868, Buddhist temples were the centers of community life, suppliers of primary education, maintainers of vital records (and tax rolls), and source of welfare assistance. Even today they continue to play active roles in their communities, especially in rural areas.

Memorial services and funerals are such important Buddhist functions that they are separately described in other questions below. Some of the other activities are briefly discussed here.

SUTRA-READING SESSIONS
Buddhist sutras often use special pronunciations not encountered in ordinary Japanese and even use Chinese characters not generally used in

Japanese. Study of the sutras thus must include not only the meaning of
the words but the pronunciations as well.

A typical sutra-reading meeting starts with incense offering by the priest and the chanting in unison of one or two sutras, then chanting of a general dedication of that reading to all beings. Sutras selected for reading are those that are recommended for laypeople to use in home devotions and any that may be especially appropriate for the particular temple. If the temple's main image is a figure of Kannon Bodhisattva, for example, sutras relating to Kannon may be emphasized.

Following the chanting by all persons present, the priest leading the session gives a short lecture on the meaning of one of the day's sutras and perhaps comments on some of the unusual characters or pronunciations used in that sutra.

The session typically concludes with tea and conversation.

SUTRA-COPYING SESSIONS

Meetings to write copies of a sutra follow a pattern similar to that of the sutra-reading sessions. The session opens with an incense offering by the priest, chanting in unison of the sutra to be copied (usually the Maka Hannya Haramitta Shingyō, called the Heart Sutra in English), and chanting of the general dedication of that reading. All the members then prepare their ink, rubbing an ink stick on a stone with a few drops of water. A printed copy of the sutra, written in well-shaped characters, is placed on the table in front of each person. A sheet of Japanese paper is neatly laid on top of the model. Writing then proceeds in silence. Each copy is dedicated in the way a sutra reading is dedicated, to the honor of a buddha or a person. All are gathered at the end of the writing and presented on the altar.

When the copies are completed, there may be a lecture by the priest. The session normally concludes with tea and conversation.

BUDDHIST MUSIC PRACTICE

Most Buddhist sects have a form of singing to the accompaniment of gongs and bells, called *go-eika*. During services for all temple members (at Obon, on the day of the founder's memorial, at the spring and fall equinox days, for example), and during individual family memorial services as well, the singers contribute to the occasion.

Practice sessions, usually held once or twice each month, not only provide a time for new members to learn the songs and older members to refresh their memories, but are social events as well. Typically the practice session starts with everyone seated on the tatami with music book, gong, striker, and bell properly arranged on a rectangular cloth placed in front of the knees. The members chant together such texts as the Four Bodhisattva Vows and the Heart Sutra, then the rehearsal begins. Go-eika, like most Japanese music, is written in its own special notation that shows the pitch of each note relative to the others but sets no absolute pitch. The leader must be sure to start each song at a pitch that will place the entire song within the comfortable singing range of all the members. New (to some or all of the group) songs are taught by the leader, one line at a time. The leader sings the line, then the group repeats that line. When the first line seems to have impressed itself on the group, the procedure is repeated for the second line, and then for the first two lines together. Once the singing has been mastered, the group proceeds to the pattern of gong strokes and bell rings during the song. I have heard a long-established group of more than fifty members strike their gongs and ring their bells in perfect unison throughout their songs, a remarkable accomplishment when one considers that there is no other accompaniment and the rhythm is not always strong or particularly regular.

The practice closes with another brief chant and rewrapping of the books and instruments (in a stringently prescribed sequence, of course). Then it is time for tea and snacks (brought by the members) and conversation. Most of the members of such groups are women in their sixties or older, many of them widows, who may live alone or are alone in the house most of the day. Temple meetings such as this provide an important opportunity for enjoying the company of other people like themselves and being part of a defined community.

2. What do the drums, gongs, and bells during services signify?

The instruments sounded during Buddhist services serve primarily to unify the chanting of sutras and to coordinate the actions of participating priests. When morning sutras are chanted by the solitary resident priest, there is no problem of unification and coordination. When the same sutras are chanted by ten or twenty ordained priests plus a hundred trainees, however, close coordination is an absolute necessity.

The wooden drum is said to be shaped like a fish, so it is called a "wooden fish"—*mokugyo*. Sutras that are read in Chinese or (greatly modified) Indic languages may have either one or two syllables per beat, unlike texts read in Japanese with a single syllable per silent beat at all times. The beat of the wooden drum provides a steady rhythm and tempo, marking each character in Chinese readings and each word in Indic readings. When a large number of people merge their voices to the beat of the drum, each using a tone comfortable for the individual, the effect is that of choral singing.

A fixed bell and handbells are struck during the entry of the main group of priests and trainees, with one or two handbells joining in as the officiating priest approaches and enters the central area of the hall. The time for bowing in unison is marked by a handbell or the smaller of the two gongs used in chanting.

Signals also rely on the two gongs. For example, a priest strikes the large gong when the officiating priest bows in front of the altar and starts to return to the central kneeling mat or platform. If the other priests are to be seated during the chanting, the small gong is struck twice just after the large gong, and everyone except the officiating priest sits down. In general, the large gong sounds to mark the officiating priest's motions, such as going forward to offer incense, returning to the center position, and bowing. The small gong is generally a signal for motion by the other priests. In readings that may continue, either repeating a single sutra several times or going from one portion of a long sutra into the next portion of that sutra, the double sounding of the small gong near the end informs everyone that chanting will halt when the end of the repetition or portion is reached. Omission of that double sounding, on the contrary, signals that the chanting will continue.

Although sutra books contain symbols for use of the gongs, in fact the sounding of the gongs should be timed to the actions of the officiating priest. A stroke of the large gong, for example, should precisely coincide with the bowing action of the officiating priest; the priest striking the gongs must watch closely for the start of a bowing motion and strike the gong accordingly. A single striking of a gong may cue separate actions of half a dozen priests assigned to specific functions, as well as the unified actions of all the remaining priests.

When I chant the morning sutras alone, or even with Taisōji's resident priest, there is no need for such elaborate coordination, but I strike the wooden drum and the gongs anyway, as is customary, using the cue symbols in the sutra book if there is no one else to act as officiating priest. It seems to me that the sounds are saying that I would go to the altar and offer incense, or make a series of bows to the floor, if it were possible to perform those actions while continuing to strike the wooden drum and the gongs.

3. What sutras are chanted in Zen temples?

Strictly speaking, a sutra is a record of the words spoken by Shakyamuni Buddha, memorized by his disciples, and finally written down after several generations of preservation through oral repetition. The basic Sanskrit word *sūtra* means a string or thread. Brahmanic sutras predating Buddhism started with important words or phrases that were strung together, as flowers in a garland, for easy repetition and memorization. Although written language existed in India before the time of the Buddha, religious teachings were considered too important and too sacred to be written down. Teachings were preserved by oral repetition performed, at least part of the time, in chorus so that discrepant versions would not so easily arise and continue.

Buddhism continued in this tradition. Soon after the death of Shakyamuni Buddha, a grand council was convened by his disciples to establish among themselves the wording of the sutras to be preserved as words spoken by the Buddha or spoken by one of his disciples and accepted by the Buddha as reflecting his own teachings. One of the reasons for regular meetings among the basically solitary Buddhist clerics was ensuring that the oral teachings were correctly preserved and transmitted to new generations.

From this start, the term sutra has come, over the centuries, to be used for any Buddhist text that has been widely accepted as accurately presenting the essence of Buddhism.

Using this extended definition of sutra, Sōtōshū regulations list the following general Buddhist texts for use in Sōtōshū temples: Perfection of Wisdom (Hannya) texts, Lotus (Hokke) texts, Flower Garland (Kegon) texts, Nirvana (Nehan) texts, "other Mahayana texts," "various *dharanis*" (Indic texts transliterated, rather than translated, into Chinese), and "various *gathas*" (verses, usually brief). In addition, certain texts by Sōtōshū priests, especially Dōgen Zenji and Keizan Zenji as founders of Sōtōshū, are read, as are several texts by Chinese priests in the Ts'ao-tung lineage in which Sōtōshū originated. Rinzaishū and Ōbakushū use much

the same texts but substitute Japanese and Chinese texts of Rinzai-lineage
priests and, for Ōbakushū, add the Sutra of Amida Buddha.

The sutras listed in the general Buddhist text collection are used at least in part by nearly all of Japan's Buddhist sects.

4. What is a Zen funeral like?

It was the Zen sects that set the pattern most widely observed today for the funerals of laypeople. Although many differences exist in the sequence of elements, number of priests involved, and inclusion of special local elements, the basic pattern is the same. The funeral described below is a Sōtōshū funeral as conducted in Tokyo.

Within hours after the death, relatives of the deceased inform the resident priest of the temple in which the deceased was a member. The resident priest arranges to meet with the relatives and to perform a sutra reading. This reading is performed directly in front of, and is dedicated to, the deceased. Family members and close friends offer incense during the reading to express their respect.

There are then five major portions of the funeral rites, three of which may be performed either at the home of the deceased, at the temple, or at a public hall designed for funerals. In earlier days, most funerals took place in the home, with the temple used only if a large number of mourners were expected to attend. With today's high rate of apartment living, however, home funerals pose problems of both physical arrangements and feelings of other residents of the building. This has done much to give rise to special funeral halls, either in the grounds of a temple or as separate buildings used for the funerals of many different temples and sects. Because embalming is not customary in Japan (the body openings are packed and dry ice is used to maintain a low temperature), the funeral rites generally start no more than two days after the day of death.

First of the major rites is the Evening of Crossing ceremony. As the name suggests, it is held in the evening, making it easier for business associates, those associated through other activities, and neighbors to attend. The "Crossing" in the name refers to the journey the deceased has made from the shore of the living to the shore of the dead, which are viewed as two sides of the same river. One to three priests chant an invocation to the bodhisattva of compassion, then chant a rather long sutra that preserves the final teachings given by Shakyamuni Buddha on his deathbed.

Because the Last Teachings Sutra is chanted in Japanese, though quite formal and old-fashioned Japanese, the listeners are provided with an opportunity to hear important Buddhist ideas explained in a straightforward fashion. During the chanting, the priest is seated immediately in front of the coffin, which usually is backed by a special altar, and the immediate family members are seated on the two sides of the priest. Other attendees enter the funeral room in turn to offer incense in respect to the deceased, then exit the room. The chanting requires about forty-five minutes and may be lengthened if there are many mourners in attendance so that all those present will have time to offer incense during the chanting. It is common for several of the mourners to join the family members after this Evening of Crossing to offer condolences. A light meal of, for example, sushi may be shared at this time.

If the funeral is being held in a temple, the immediate family members normally stay overnight at the temple, remaining close to the deceased. In the home, of course, they are there already.

The funeral itself is held the next day, usually starting sometime between 9:00 A.M. and 1:00 P.M. The timing is purely practical: cremation is almost universal, and in Tokyo the cremation normally takes place immediately following the funeral. The funeral schedule, therefore, must take into account the schedule at the cremation facility. Cremation facilities are in operation five days of every six. A Chinese cycle of six daily fortunes, designating each day as auspicious or inauspicious for certain activities, was imported to Japan and remains in common use. Weddings are most often scheduled for "great peace" days, an auspicious time for any new start. Funerals are almost never held on "pulling along a friend" days because of the implication that the deceased may "pull along" friends or family into death. Days of the "pulling friend" designation thus are closing days for cremation facilities and days when Buddhist priests can schedule group activities with confidence that no one will be absent because of having to perform a funeral.

What is commonly referred to as the funeral is, in fact, two separate (and separable in time) rites: the funeral proper and the "leave-taking" ceremony. In the case of public figures, the leave-taking ceremony portion may be performed a week or more after the funeral portion, allowing time to organize a large gathering. Usually, however, the leave-taking ceremony begins the instant the funeral proper concludes.

The funeral proper is the ceremony of giving the Buddhist precepts to a layperson. This custom originated in Japan. During medieval times, wealthy patrons of major temples were impressed with the rites performed following the death of a cleric. Wishing to receive that level of reverence themselves, at first they established a custom of entering the Buddhist clergy late in life, or when an accident or illness threatened death. The custom gradually expanded to include people from all walks of life, and the receiving of the precepts was shifted from during the person's lifetime to following death. Living in accordance with the precepts is accepted as an ideal way of life; those who were unable to follow that path during life are viewed as having nonetheless wished to do so. The posthumous giving of the precepts thus becomes a fulfillment of the presumed continuing wish of the deceased.

The officiating priest symbolically shaves the head of the deceased, reciting the verse for purification that accompanies head shaving. Then the acceptance-of-responsibility verse is read by the officiating priest and echoed by the assisting priest(s). Water is sprinkled by the officiating priest to complete the symbolic purification of both giver and receiver of the precepts. The precepts are then conferred. First, the Three Refuges (my life is founded in the Buddha; my life is founded in the Buddhist teachings; my life is founded in the community of Buddhists). Then the Three Pure Precepts (refrain from what promotes evil; do what promotes good; act so as to benefit others). Lastly, the Ten Grave Prohibitions (not to kill; not to steal; not to engage in wrongful sexual activity; not to lie; not to encourage use of intoxicants; not to speak ill of others; not to praise oneself, and not to be too proud to praise others; not to covet either dharma or property; not to give way to anger; and not to disparage the "three treasures"—the Buddha, dharma, and sangha).

The precepts having been transmitted from the officiating priest to the deceased, the officiating priest confers a chart showing the line of precepts transmission from Shakyamuni Buddha to the officiating priest, then the deceased (now invested with a new "precepts name"), and circling back to Shakymuni Buddha in token of the interconnectedness of all causes and effects. The precepts name is henceforth used in sutra dedications, on the memorial plaque, and on the gravestone. The lineage chart is later placed in the top of the urn containing the cremated bones.

This completed, several sutras are chanted and dedicated to the honor of the deceased. This concludes the funeral itself.

The leave-taking ceremony starts with a sermon by the officiating priest that lauds the deceased and includes a Chinese-style poem designed to lead the deceased into the peace of the "other shore" of those no longer in this imperfect world. Representative mourners may offer words of remembrance, appreciation, and farewell to the deceased, and telegrams of condolence to the family often are read. Upon conclusion of these speeches, the priests once more chant sutras dedicated to the deceased. During this portion of the ceremony (and indeed usually throughout the funeral as well), those attending enter the ceremony hall in turn and offer incense to show respect to the deceased.

With the funeral and leave-taking ceremony concluded, the coffin is removed from the funeral altar and opened so that each attendee may place a flower in the coffin and make a farewell to the deceased. When all have done this, each member of the immediate family aids in closing the coffin lid with nails, a task that is completed by those responsible for the physical arrangements. The coffin is then placed in a hearse, the main body of which is shaped and decorated like an elaborate lacquered coffin, and carried to the cremation facility. Ordinarily it is only the family members and a priest who accompany the deceased through the remainder of the rites.

At the cremation facility, family members and priest gather to see the coffin placed inside the cremation unit, then each person once more offers incense. During the hour or so required for cremation, everyone waits in a separate room. By this time, the immediate family members are usually tired and concerned about all the things that remain to be done in connection with the death. I have often felt that having a foreigner with them presents a diversion that is probably welcome. At one cremation, the half-dozen members of the immediate family left their places at a table and went around the room greeting the others present, pouring beer or tea for them. As the first one returned and sat down, he asked me how long I had been in Japan. I answered it was almost twenty years. We exchanged another sentence or two, then the second one returned to the table. Number two asked, "How long have you been in Japan?" I repeated the answer. As numbers three and four returned, we repeated this ritual, so by the time number five reached the table and started to ask, all the others said in chorus "She's been here twenty years." It was the first occasion for smiles that day, and probably the first in three days or more.

When the cremation has been completed, everyone goes to witness removal of the remains from the cremation unit. The bones, for that is what endures through the cremation, are moved to a tray beside the waiting urn. Two by two, family members use long wooden chopsticks to lift a bone and place it in the urn. The transfer starts with the foot bones and proceeds upward. Meantime the priest is usually reciting a sutra in praise of the Buddha's relics. A crematorium employee sets aside the skull and jaw bone before the other bones are moved. When everyone present has helped to place a bone in the urn, the employee uses small utensils to slide all the remaining bones into the urn at once. This brisk practicality always seems to me to be greatly at odds with the ritualized actions that precede it. The jaw bones and skull go on top, and over them goes the lineage chart, showing that the deceased received the precepts from a priest in a continuous lineage back to Shakyamuni Buddha, thus linking the deceased directly to the Buddha.

The sequence is almost finished. Everyone returns to the temple, bearing the urn of bones neatly enclosed in a wooden box, white wrapper, and brocade cover. Two brief services, normally with only one sutra each, are performed. One is an expression that now the deceased has reached the condition of peace, of nirvana. The other is the seventh-day memorial service. It is likely that not all those present will be able to attend another service on the exact seventh day after the death, so that memorial service is often conducted twice, once following the cremation and again on the real seventh day.

There is usually a meal for everyone at the temple as a way of showing the chief mourner's appreciation to all who participated in the long day of services. The day concludes with the chief mourner carrying home the urn and the standing plaque with the precepts name, to be placed on the family altar until seven weeks have passed (at which time the urn is placed in the family tomb).

5. What is a Buddhist grave like?

Visitors to Japan are often surprised at the small size of cemetery plots. Gravestones seem packed in everywhere. They are even more astonished to learn that each plot holds not just the remains of one person but those of an entire family. This is particularly notable in city cemeteries. The reason is the custom of cremation rather than whole body burial. Cremation is almost universal in Japan.

Figure 12 shows a typical grave plot. Although this shows a rather large area, often the entire plot is barely larger than the tombstone itself. The upright stone at the back is engraved with the family name on the front

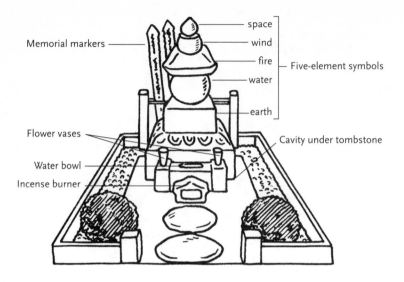

Memorial markers

space
wind
fire
water
earth

Five-element symbols

Flower vases

Water bowl

Incense burner

Cavity under tombstone

Figure 12. Family grave with five-elements tombstone

and has precepts names, death dates, names, and ages at death of individual family members listed on the back. Below the tombstone there is a cavity in the earth, often with a shelf across the rear portion, about halfway up from the base of the cavity. In Tokyo, the urn containing the cremated bones is placed on that shelf, together with the urns for other family members who have died recently. Fundamentally, though, Japanese Buddhists speak of their "bones becoming the earth." When the memorial cycle has been completed (or when the shelf becomes full of urns), the remains are transferred from the urn to the soil beneath the tombstone, to be united with the earth itself. Although the remains are individual bones and bone fragments immediately after cremation, when they are placed in the urn, over time they crumble into powder, and it is this powder that joins the earth. In some areas, the cremated remains are immediately placed directly on the base of the cavity instead of being kept in an urn for many years.

The incense burner and flower vase structures are movable, and the stone slab below them can be pried up and moved to one side. This offers access to the cavity below, for interment of a recently deceased family member.

At the time of interment, when a memorial service is held, and on the occasions of the spring and autumn equinoxes and the summer Obon

ceremony, family members visit the grave to pay respect to those interred
there. They offer flowers and burn incense. Each person then bows before
the grave, takes a dipper of water from a bucket and pours the water over
the tombstone, allowing it to settle into the shallow water bowl carved
between the bases for flower vases, and concludes with another bow to the
memory of the deceased.

6. What is a Zen memorial service?

"Memorial service" is the term generally used in English for the series of
formal remembrances of the deceased that is a special characteristic of
Japanese Buddhism. Sutra-chanting observances to signify respect and
appreciation for the dead start on the day of the funeral and continue, in
many cases, for as long as thirty-six or even forty-nine years.

There are three general memorial occasions each year in addition to
the series of services for individual persons. The three general occasions—
spring and fall Ohigan, on the vernal and autumnal equinoxes, and the
late-summer Obon—are described as part of the Buddhist holidays discussed under the question "What are the main Buddhist holidays marked
by temples?" Here, I will describe the services for individual persons,
which are attended not only by family members but also by friends and
associates of the person being remembered. These services are an occasion
for all those affected by the life of the deceased to recall and appreciate the
influences on their own lives.

The series starts with the day of the funeral. Next come the first
through seventh weeks after death. In the Tokyo area and many others,
the urn containing the bones of the deceased is placed in the family grave
at the end of the seventh-week memorial service. Another memorial takes
place one hundred days after the death, and there is one held one year after
the death. The remaining memorial services are called the third, seventh,
thirteenth, seventeenth, twenty-third, twenty-seventh, thirty-third, thirty-
seventh, and fiftieth annual memorials. It is sometimes said that the series
should last until no one in the family remembers how to pronounce the
precepts name of the deceased. In practice, precepts names are rarely *that*
obscure. The saying, though, reflects the general principle that memorial
services express the appreciation of those who knew the deceased and thus
continue only while there are family members living who can remember
the person memorialized.

The sequence was first described to me as "first-year death anniversary, third-year death anniversary, and so forth." I was surprised, therefore, when temple members whose son had died very young remarked to me that it hardly seemed possible that we had reached the seventh memorial. It indeed seemed hardly possible to me that seven years had passed, and I later discovered that they hadn't. My enlightenment on that subject, though, came only after my mother's death. I was a bit startled when Taisōji's resident priest added a memorial service for my mother to our zazen group's morning sutras just two years after her death, as I had asked him to do for the one-year memorial. The following year, I asked him to hold a service later in the day when two of my priest friends could also participate. He, in turn, seemed a bit surprised but readily agreed. When it got to be six years after my mother's death, the resident priest announced to me in January that "This March will be the seventh memorial for your mother." I thought my mind must be playing tricks on me, so I went home and checked the year of her death. Sure enough, it had only been six years! Then I thought to look at the chart of memorial years posted to remind temple members of the schedule. Lo and behold, the year of death that corresponded to the current year's seventh memorial service was only six years earlier. The count of "occasions" or "annual memorials" starts, I discovered, with "one" for the day of the funeral. (Until about fifty years ago, Japanese were said to be one year old at birth.) The third memorial thus occurs two years after the death, and so on.

This, I might note, is a cautionary tale for those who uncritically accept the terms used in English by Japanese Buddhist priests or even by American or other English-speaking Buddhist priests who learned them from Japanese priests. Someone, sometime, suggests an English term such as "death anniversary," and everyone else soon uses it without pausing to consider its meaning.

The services themselves are identical, regardless of which occasion has been reached. At Taisōji, in a typical pattern, the officiating priest offers incense and announces the occasion of the service, then returns to the central position and kneels on the cushion there to chant sutras. The officiating and assisting priests chant one sutra and proceed into another. At this time the officiating priest offers powdered incense once more and, upon returning to the central cushion, invites the people attending the service to go forward and offer incense in turn. Meanwhile the second sutra is continuing and a third is started if need be. When everyone has offered incense and the second (or third) sutra has come to its end, the dedication of the sutra reading to the memory of the deceased (whose precepts name is used) is read by the officiating priest and assisting priest. The officiating priest returns to the altar for a final incense offering, announces that the memorial service has been performed, and thanks the people attending the service. After the priests have left the hall, the laypeople leave and usually proceed to the grave, where they offer flowers and incense and pour water over the gravestone. Often they all return to the temple for a meal together before going their separate ways home.

Put so straightforwardly, the whole thing sounds very dull. In practice, there often is a good deal of drama involved, especially for the priests. Temples with several hundred member families, all of whom want their family memorial services conducted on a Sunday (though in recent years Saturday has also become acceptable), end by performing five or more services in a day, with vanishingly small intervals between. During those intervals, the priests must replace the name in the stand on the altar, remove any offerings of fruit, sweets, or other such items brought for the previous service, arrange and install on the altar any offerings of fruit, sweets, flowers, or other items brought for the next service, install the wooden memorial markers (symbolic of temples) dedicated to the next person memorialized, and persuade those attending the next service to enter the hall and seat themselves. Preferably in an area for sitting down, not in the corridor that the officiating priest must use to enter and exit the hall. And certainly not on the ledge of the tokonoma alcove as one family did, to my considerable shock. Inasmuch as seating is viewed by all as an expression of rank within the group, and no one except the chief mourner and spouse is initially willing to sit in any position other than the last, working out places for everyone can be time-consuming. If there are enough guests to make seating space a problem, the priests can rely on at least one of them to bring another offering into the hall and thrust it upon the assisting priest only when everyone has finally settled down. The offering then must be placed on a footed stand that goes on the altar. By now, the service that was supposed to start at 11:30 has reached 11:55 without even starting. So all the remaining services will be at least twenty-five minutes late (lateness accumulates as the day goes along, just as with doctors appointments).

During later services, or those with many persons attending and thus long durations of incense offering, my feet usually go numb. Standing up at the end of the service becomes a problem. I soon learned to adjust position and prepare beforehand for standing, though, when I observed what happened to the wooden markers. These "temples" built in honor of the person memorialized are removed from the rack in the temple and carried to the grave, where they are installed in a similar rack behind the gravestone. The markers are sharply pointed at the base, which rests in a shallow groove in the temple rack, and are several feet tall. Basic support is provided by parallel horizontal bars that hold the markers between them. Tight spacing, maintained by a blocking peg, prevents lateral motion of the markers. One male guest would approach the rack and remove a marker from one end, releasing that end from the blocking peg. Another man would then invariably remove a marker from the other end. The inevitable result was that the remaining markers, completely freed in the lateral direction, fell at angles to each other and occasionally even slipped out of the base. This procedure was one I considered both noisy and unaesthetic. So I learned to prepare my numb feet for leaping up and running to the rack as soon as the officiating priest exited (or, if I was officiating, as soon as I had concluded the service). I then could hold off my would-be "helpers" by thrusting markers at them while I continued supporting and removing the remaining markers. That safely accomplished, I had only to persuade that group of guests to exit the hall so that I could prepare the altar for the next group.

7. What "prayers" are used in Buddhist services?

Nothing that is said by either priests or laypeople during a Buddhist religious service can reasonably be interpreted as a prayer. The sutras that are chanted are the teachings of Shakyamuni Buddha and his disciples, plus those of later generations of priests. In Taisōji's morning sutra chanting, for example, the first sutra we chant begins in English (as given in *Soto Shu Sutras*, published by the Sōtōshū administrative headquarters):

> Avalokiteshvara Bodhisattva, doing deep prajna paramita,
> Clearly saw the emptiness of all the five conditions,
> Thus completely relieving misfortune and pain.

A text from Sōtōshū founder Dōgen that is chanted during the funeral service starts with:

This is the most important problem of all for Buddhists.

It ends with:

> Understand that in this life you have only one life, not two or
> three. How regrettable it is if, fruitlessly holding false views, you
> vainly do wrong, thinking that you are not doing bad when, in
> fact, you are. You cannot avoid the karmic retribution of your evil
> acts even though you mistakenly assume that because you do not
> recognize its existence you are not subject to it.

The general dedication for sutra readings, often used by both priests
and laypeople, is translated in the same book as:

> May the merit of this penetrate
> Into each thing in all places
> So that we and every sentient being
> Together can realize the Buddha's Way.

> The ten directions, the three worlds, all Buddhas;
> All venerable ones, Bodhisattvas, Mahasattvas;
> The great Prajna Paramita.

My own quite literal translation of the dedication used in Sōtōshū
memorial services, intended for understanding but not for recitation, is:

> The world is completely pure and full of light
> That shines, embracing the universe.
> When we look at our world,
> It seems the stuff of dreams.
> What we hope, as we bow before the Buddha, Buddhist law,
>   and community of Buddhist adherents,
> Is that we may see that brightness.
> We humbly meet in this temple, this month and this day,
> To honor [precepts name of the person memorialized] on the
>   occasion of [the event for which the memorial service is held;
>   for example, the seventh day after death].
> We respectfully offer incense, flowers, and candlelight,
> And the chanting of the [name of the sutra] for this occasion,

Encouraging the awakened spirit and magnifying the place of reward.

Bowing low, we make a vow, acting in the flow of life and death,
While the priceless jewel (seeing reality) shines alone in the blue sea,
And spreads throughout the shore of awakening and non-awakening,
As the shining wheel (seeing reality) spins serenely alone in the blue heaven,
That we shall lead the wide world of people
All to follow the paths of awakening.

That is what is so often described in English as "ancestor worship" or, alternatively, as "praying for the repose of the soul."

No, there definitely are no prayers, and no ancestor worship, involved in Buddhist religious services.

8. What is the meaning of the beads that Buddhists use?

In the Zen sects, strings of beads called *o-juzu* are held by the officiating priest during memorial services, funerals, and special services. The beads are rubbed both to symbolize freedom of the deceased from the numberless desires and attachments of human life and to symbolically transfer the good act of chanting sutras from the priest to the person memorialized. Laypeople hold similar, usually shorter, strings of beads circling the fingers of both hands and held with both thumbs while they are offering incense and bowing to a buddha or bodhisattva or to a person memorialized. In this case, the symbolism is primarily that of performing good actions out of respect for the buddha, bodhisattva, or deceased person.

A complete string of beads, as held by an officiating priest, is 108 beads plus 1 that secures the two ends of the cord and often 5 that divide the total into six groups of 18 beads each. The beads often are seeds of the bodhi tree, though wood, ceramic, glass, and crystal beads also are used. The priest wears these beads around the left wrist or holds them in the left hand when not actively using them. My count of beads on the full strand that I use when acting as officiating priest shows exactly 108 regular beads, plus 1 end bead and 5 divider beads. A metal ring, much larger in diameter than the beads, slides freely along the strand when the beads move with my hand or when I rub two sections of the strand together, making the motion slightly audible.

Laypeople rarely use the full 108-bead length. Instead they wear fractional lengths, such as 27 (one-fourth), 36 (one-third), or 54 (one-half) beads. There seems to be a fad among Japanese young men for wearing Buddhist beads, generally in the one-fourth length and strung on elastic cord. One young priest I know habitually wears two such strands of beads so that he can give one strand to any acquaintance who may ask for one. Those obtained from a priest are, I gather, considered the "real thing" as opposed to just any strand of beads in about that length.

Different Buddhist sects use different types of beads. In Pure Land sects, the beads are fashioned for counting repetitions of the phrase *Namu Amida Butsu*, or "I pay reverence to Amida Buddha." Unlike the Catholic rosary, Buddhist beads have no specific texts associated with them and are seldom used in a way that associates beads with any text.

9. In Japan, Zen and other Buddhist priests traditionally officiate at funerals, but weddings are usually done by Shinto priests. Is there such a ceremony as a Zen wedding?

Yes, there is a ceremony prescribed by Sōtōshū, and I assume there are similar ceremonies for Rinzaishū and Ōbakushū. Having been a guest at two Sōtōshū weddings and assisting priest for another two such weddings, I probably have more experience in that area than most Sōtōshū priests.

One of the weddings where I assisted was that of an American bride and a Japanese groom. For the sake of the bride and of her parents, who could not come to Tokyo for the wedding, I translated the sequence of events in the marriage service. It was as follows:

1. Entrance of bride and groom
2. Entrance of officiating priest
3. Opening words by officiating priest
4. Reading of ceremony statement
5. Sprinkling of water on bride's and groom's heads to confer wisdom

6. Presentation to bride and groom of Buddhist beads and wedding rings

7. Chanting by all of the Three Refuges (my life is founded in the Buddha; my life is founded in the Buddhist teachings; my life is founded in the community of Buddhists)

8. Vows by the bride and groom

9. Address by officiating priest

10. Chanting by all of the Four Vows of a Bodhisattva (we vow to bring all the innumerable beings to the shore of awakening; we vow to extinguish the inexhaustible delusions; we vow to master the immeasurable teachings; we vow to follow the endless path of the Buddha)

11. Closing words

Both the officiating priest's words and the vows by bride and groom concentrate on loving and caring for each other, each considering the needs of the other, those of the children who will (it is hoped) be born, and those of the parents of both spouses.

Religious ceremonies for weddings were rare until the twentieth century. Before that, weddings were marked by various actions on the part of the spouses and their families, and by registration of the marriage into the residence rolls of the locality. The inclusion of a religious service was urged upon Japanese by Christian missionaries, who viewed Japanese as having an excessive rate of divorce.

10. Why does Zen include ancestor worship?

It doesn't. A family gathering to remember a deceased relative, probably on the birth anniversary rather than the death anniversary, or the provision of special flowers in memory of someone for a regular church service, is not considered "ancestor worship" when it occurs in the West. Why, then, is a somewhat more organized version of the same thing termed "ancestor worship" when it occurs in Japan?

As noted in the section on "What is a Zen memorial service?" the service is held to remember the deceased. Both family members (not only descendants, but relations of all sorts) and friends and associates take the occasion to recall the role that the deceased played in their lives. They express gratitude for their interactions during the life of the deceased. The formal dedication of the sutras chanted at the service simply says that life and death are the two shores of a single river, with death being the shore of nirvana that we all hope to reach in time.

One basic feeling about ancestors in Japan, arising before the introduction of Buddhism and continuing in some ways right down to the present, is that the dead may become malevolent spirits, causing all kinds of misfortunes both public and private. During the early stages of belief in such spirits, only nobles or local leaders could wreak vengeance after death. With the coming of Buddhism and its egalitarian concepts, however, the field of possible malevolent spirits was widened to include common people. On whom would a common person impose vengeance? On family members, and especially on direct descendants. The same actions that are used to show appreciation to family members who have died are therefore also used to guard against any interference by those dead members in the affairs of the living.

11. Why is there no music in Zen temples?

Some temples often have choral music, of a special Buddhist variety, during services, and a few temples use musical chanting for certain services. In general, sutra chanting is used as a form of music in place of, or in addition to, these other forms. Sutra chanting should be performed in a singing voice, singing on a single tone, rather than a speaking voice. Each person uses a single tone that is comfortable.

Buddhist choral music is called go-eika. That translates literally as "sacred songs." It is performed mostly by laypeople, singing a melody in unison to the accompaniment of small gongs and handbells. Each singer has a small handbell and a small metal gong, which is struck with a wooden hammer. The instruments, like the singing itself, must be in perfect unison. The go-eika group may sing at the beginning and end of a service, and usually sings during the period when laypeople offer incense. Members of go-eika groups are almost all women, and middle-aged or older women predominate. In fact, group members are widely referred to as "the go-eika grandmothers." The songs are written in a notation system that gives only relative pitch; there is no symbol for, say, middle C, but instead there are symbols for do, re, mi, etc. in three octaves (basic, one above, and one below). The length of the pitch-symbol line indicates the duration, and triangles and circles show the points at which the gong and bell should sound.

Musical chanting of sutras, called *shōmyō* ("shining voice"), is performed by priests. Each sect has its own special variety of shōmyō, just as each has its own go-eika. A different notation system is used, but again it is one based on relative pitch rather than absolute notes and again the singing is entirely in unison with no harmony used.

Both these forms of vocal music emphasize cooperation and flexibility. The leader must set the initial pitch at a level allowing all members to sing through the entire song. All members must work for perfect unity in their singing. Buddhist music, as so much of Japanese Buddhism, shows centuries of interaction with Japanese customs and sensibilities.

12. How does someone get a Buddhist name, and when do people use their Buddhist names?

A Buddhist name is customarily given to a person who receives the Buddhist precepts. Receiving the precepts may occur upon entry into the priesthood, as a formal pledge to follow the precepts as a layperson, or, in by far the most common case, as part of the funeral ceremony. As noted under "What is a Zen funeral like?" the funeral proper is a precepts ceremony. It is assumed that the deceased wanted to receive and uphold the precepts in life but was hindered by circumstances. The name given as part of the funeral is called a "precepts name"—in Japanese, *kaimyō*. Those given to the living are called dharma names—*hōmyō*. Not long after my entry into the priesthood as a trainee, the priest I apprenticed to announced my new status to a zazen group he led. One woman in the group promptly asked, "Oh, is Jiho her kaimyō?" There was a rather shocked silence before he replied that although it *is* a precepts name, a kaimyō, that term is not normally used for a living person.

Whatever the occasion for receiving the precepts, the name given at that time usually consists of three elements, each of which consists of two Chinese characters. The first element is called a *gō* and functions in place of a family name. My gō, for example, is Zuian. The second element is the dharma name or precepts name proper, which functions as a given name. Most Japanese priests legally change their given names to their dharma names upon entry into the priesthood, although some delay that change for many years and some never make the legal change. My dharma name, Jiho, appears on my Japanese alien registration card and I use it in daily life. The third element is a rank. A layperson receiving the precepts may be given a name with the rank omitted. In a precepts name received after death, a common rank is *shinji* ("gentleman adherent") or *shinnyo* ("gentlewoman adherent"). Priests hold various ranks as they progress through their training sequence.

The combination of the first two elements is used by priests on a few formal occasions, such as giving the precepts to a lay adherent. The dharma name, as noted, often becomes the legal given name of a priest. Given names of the sons of a priest, especially the eldest son, often are chosen to be convertible to dharma names just by changing the pronunciation, leaving the Chinese characters the same. For the dead, the complete precepts name is always used on the memorial plaque and memorial markers, on the tombstone, and in dedications of sutra readings. Living laypeople, however, rarely use their dharma names. The dharma name of a priest or layperson, by the way, becomes the precepts name used after death.

There has been quite a lot of media attention in recent years to the practice by a few priests of assigning very elaborate precepts names not only to people who have been particularly devoted to Buddhism, as is the accepted custom, but also to those whose heirs make a large donation to the temple at the time of the funeral. Admittedly that is one solution to covering the cost of, for example, a new roof on the temple. The families want a precepts name that sounds especially good because from the funeral onward, that is the name that will appear on the memorial plaque in the family altar, carved into the family tombstone, written on memorial markers erected at the grave following memorial services, and spoken by the priest during memorial services. It becomes not just a private matter but an indication of family status. Many priests I know have now made it a habit to explain to the family arranging a funeral that they will not accept any donations related to the level of precepts name they assign, so as to avoid attempts by families to seek special names. In the Buddhist teachings (as opposed to popular imagination), every precepts receiver is a treasured member of the community of adherents; such elements as the length of the name and the rank used are only a means of expressing appreciation by the priest and temple as a whole for the lifelong efforts of the deceased in furthering temple activities and Buddhism.

13. Why should Westerners chant in Japanese?

In my experience, Western laypeople rarely *do* chant in Japanese, even though their chanting may not be in a Western language. Even Japanese laypeople have few occasions to chant in Japanese. The reason for this helps to explain the situation, I think.

There are two basic varieties of chanting used in Japanese Buddhism. The first, most often heard and used, variety consists of chanting to the beat of a wooden drum (mokugyō). There are two subtypes of this variety. In the first subtype, one Chinese character, which may be pronounced in one or two syllables, is read for each beat of the drum. The actual language used in this case is Chinese, albeit with pronunciations modified by history and adaptation to Japanese speech habits. Examples of this kind of chanting include the Heart Sutra and the Lotus Sutra (Myōhōrengekyō), both widely used in Zen daily services. (The Lotus Sutra is so long that only one chapter, or only the verse portion of one chapter, is generally chanted; chapter 16 ["Nyorai Juryōhon"] and chapter 25 ["Kanzeon Bosatsu Fumonbon"] are the most-often selected.) In the second type, one Indic word is read for each beat of the drum. A single Indic word may be presented as one or two Chinese characters. These are the dharanis, described in more detail below. Perhaps the most popular example is the Dharani of the Great Compassionate One (Daihishin Darani).

The second basic variety of chanting is that used for chanting that is, in fact, done in Japanese. Nothing is used to mark the beat in this form of chanting. Each syllable of the Japanese text is given equal length and stress. One example is Dōgen's *Fukanzazengi* (General Advice on the Principles of Zazen).

Neither of these patterns is suited to chanting in English or European languages. One might argue on aesthetic grounds that if the language is to be changed, the method of chanting should also be changed to suit the "new" language. At least one Western Zen group, Shasta Abbey and its affiliates, uses plainsong for chanting in English; the result is a matching of method and language that is much easier to learn and pleasanter to hear than is the clash produced by attempting English with equalized length and stress for each syllable.

It is worth noting that although Buddhism reached Japan in the sixth century, Indic and Chinese languages are used by Japanese for sutra chanting to this day. Doesn't this fourteen-century preservation of earlier sutra

languages argue that a bit more time might be taken to decide that everything should be chanted in Western languages?

The case of dharanis is especially interesting. When Buddhism entered China, its sacred texts were quickly translated into Chinese. Taoist terminology was widely used at that time (just as Christian terminology is widely used in today's translations into Western languages) on the assumption that a familiar vocabulary would make it easy for China's people to understand the new religion. Predictably, what happened was that Buddhist doctrines were greatly distorted and Buddhism was popularly perceived as merely a foreign offshoot of the native Chinese teachings.

Some three centuries later, the situation began to be corrected when Tao-an, a Chinese Buddhist cleric who studied widely with Buddhist clerics from India and Central Asia, instituted a new effort to catalog the sutras known in China and to prepare new translations free from Taoist vocabulary. This effort used Tao-an's concept of "five losses and three difficulties" in translating from Indic into Chinese. The first loss originates in the reversal of word order needed to conform to Chinese grammar. The second is created in the Chinese preference for ornate, polished writing rather than the simple, unadorned style preferred by Indians. The third loss occurred when Chinese translators eliminated the repetitions of one or more sentences that were used by Indic language writers to emphasize a point or to facilitate memorization of oral literature. The fourth loss was the elimination, in Chinese translations, of explanatory material in the middle of a sentence in Indic writing. Although the introduction of passages often running more than a thousand characters into the middle of a sentence of Indic writing certainly did obscure the original point of the interrupted sentence, total elimination of the explanatory material lost the complex meaning of the original Indic text. The fifth loss was similar, caused by elimination in Chinese of the Indic repetition in a subsequent passage of an explanation that had already been fully presented.

The "three difficulties" of Tao-an were first that the graceful, highly inflected Sanskrit had to be translated into plain, comprehensible Chinese; second, that Sanskrit sentences expressing subtle nuances of Indian thought from the time of Shakyamuni Buddha had to be made clear to Chinese readers of Tao-an's era; and third, that the translators often lacked the profound knowledge of Buddhism necessary for accurate translation.

After another three centuries, Hsuan-tsang proposed "five kinds of untranslatable words" that should be simply transliterated (phonetically transcribed) from Indic-language words instead of being translated into Chinese. The first type, typified by dharanis, involved words having profound meanings that defy a single, simple translation. The language of dharanis evolved through oral repetition into patterns that made oral chanting easy and that facilitated memorization. The result was a special language that seemed to have a power beyond the literal meanings of individual words.

The remaining four types of untranslatable words were those with multiple meanings, those referring to things having no Chinese equivalent (plants, animals, minerals, and places unknown to the Chinese), those that had traditionally been transliterated over the preceding six centuries, and those that would lose their special meanings if translated into Chinese (for example, prajna, which has a meaning beyond simple "wisdom").

Before we urge instant translation of all Buddhist texts into European languages, and especially before we urge that such translations be chanted and not merely used to assist study, I think we might do well to consider the insights and experience of the Chinese translators. After all, even in modern times when Christian texts were translated from Western languages into Chinese, the ancient cautions of Tao-an and Hsuan-tsang were still observed.

14. What are the main Buddhist holidays marked by temples?

Three of the four primary holidays marked by Buddhist temples are also national holidays in Japan. The four are New Year's, the spring and autumn equinoxes, and the summer Obon period. Obon, although it is not a national holiday, is the customary period for vacation from work and school as a time for return to the family hometown.

The first three days of each new year are marked by a whole series of traditional events. Debts are repaid and the entire nation has a housecleaning spree (for offices, factories, and temples, among others, in addition to homes) in the closing days of each year so the new year can start afresh. At some time during the first week of January, most of the population pauses to make at least a quick visit to a Shinto shrine or a Buddhist temple, and many visit both. Although temples may not hold public ceremonies at this time, they are visited by members as the family goes to the cemetery for New Year's remembrance of departed family members, offering flowers and incense and pouring water over the gravestone.

The equinoxes are known in Buddhism as Ohigan, "that shore." They are times for remembering those who have crossed from "this" shore of human life to "that other shore" of the same river of universal existence. Again there are visits to the family grave, usually taking special memorial markers in addition to the standard flowers, incense, and water. The memorial markers are tall, thin strips of wood shaped at the top to represent a stupa, the original form of Buddhist temples. These are stood behind the gravestone to symbolically erect a temple in honor of the dead. One marker normally is offered in memory of all the family dead collectively. If a family member has crossed the river of existence since the previous Ohigan, a separate memorial marker probably will be offered specifically for that person. The memorial markers are prepared and dedicated by the temple's resident priest and assistant priests. Often, especially on the occasion of a "first Ohigan," there is a memorial service in the temple before the visit to the grave. Although each equinox is only one day as a physical event and as a national holiday, three days are added on each side of that day for a one-week observance in temples.

Obon is the major memorial time of the year, as well as being a harvest celebration and a time for family reunion (or nowadays, for travel overseas instead). In a reflection of varying responses to the change from lunar to solar calendar system, Obon time may occur in either July or August. For the most part, major urban areas mark the season in July whereas August is chosen in the countryside. Nothing is that simple, however, so two neighboring temples may have their observances a month or more apart. Obon is one of the rare occasions on which all the temple members gather for a collective service. That service re-creates an event described in sutras. One of Shakyamuni Buddha's close disciples had the gift of being able to see different realms of being instead of seeing only this human realm. After the death of his mother, Mokuren (the disciple) became worried about her new existence. He searched the realms of being for her and found, alas, that she had fallen into the realm of the hungry spirits. Because of her greed as a human, she had become a being with a throat too small for the tiniest grain of rice to pass through it. All beings in that realm existed in constant torture from thirst and hunger. Mokuren saw this and promptly went to Shakyamuni Buddha, asking what he could do to relieve that suffering. The Buddha's answer was that he should make food offerings to all the disciples and ask them to chant incantations dedicated to the release of all beings from that terrible realm. When Mokuren did so, he saw that his mother and the rest were freed from the realm of hungry spirits and entered one of the happier realms. (According to ancient Indian cosmology, as adapted by Buddhism, all living beings exist within the realms of desire, which include the realms inhabited by—from most to least fortunate—heavenly beings, humans, fierce powerful beings who love fighting, animals, hungry spirits, and beings of hells.) The Obon service thus features food offerings and the chanting of incantations, words of power that have been retained in their original Indic language rather than being translated, albeit modified in pronunciation by passage through Chinese and Japanese. The memorial markers dedicated during this service are later taken by each family to the cemetery and offered at the grave, together with flowers, incense, and water.

In addition to these, most temples have special observances for the birthday of Shakyamuni Buddha, celebrated in Japan on the eighth of either April or May (once more, the calendar change created a variation). These celebrations are called the Flower Festival. A special statue of the infant Buddha is placed in a bowl of sweet tea, made from hydrangea leaves, surrounded by various bright flowers. Priests and laypeople alike bow to the Buddha and pour the sweet tea over the figure in homage. Often all the temples in a local area cooperate in a single observance of this event. Children are at the center of the observance, sometimes being costumed as small bodhisattvas. It is a happy and very colorful event.

In some areas, temples arrange special displays of their treasured paintings of the Buddha's death, held during the week preceding February 15, Japan's traditional date for the entry into nirvana.

Other special observances at a temple may include those marking the deaths of the founders of the sect and of that temple; one dedicated to the Buddhist figure that is the main image in the temple; and a symbolic reading of the entire Sutra of Perfect Wisdom. This last is fascinating to watch and to hear. The six hundred volumes of the sutra are divided among several priests who then fan each volume to the right, left, then center, creating a waterfall effect with the accordion-folded pages, while chanting the volume number and a phrase from the sutra. Often this is accompanied by rapid drumming. Because a number of priests are needed for the service, temples in a district schedule their observances so that priests from all the temples can participate in all the services, just as is done for the Obon service.

"Those statues" are almost certain to be images of Jizō Bodhisattva, a bodhisattva said to protect travelers, children, and the dead. Often they wear red caps and bibs given, for the most part, by mothers in thanks for the recovery of a child from illness or injury or in memory of a child who has died. This practice has grown so popular in recent years that sometimes statues of other buddhas and bodhisattvas are also given caps. The bib, associated with infants, is less likely to appear on any statue other than Jizō, however.

Jizō Bodhisattva is much more visible in Japan than in other Buddhist countries. The figure of a traveling priest, with shaved head, travel staff, and often carrying a healing jewel, is a familiar sight on roadsides as well as in temple grounds. Within a five-minute walk from my home, there are two temples noted for their Jizō statues. One, a Shingonshū temple of the esoteric Buddhist tradition, has an outdoor statue of Jizō sitting down—a rare pose. This immense bronze image was erected by the government in 1714 to guard travelers along the Nakasendō, a main highway between the ruling centers of the period, Edo (Tokyo) where the shogunate was based and Kyoto where the imperial court was located. In all, six such travel-protection Jizōs were provided by the government for the six main highways leading out of Edo.

The other is an extremely popular Sōtōshū temple that is formally named Kōganji but is familiarly known as Togenuki Jizōdera, the temple of the thorn-pulling Jizō. The main image in this temple is a Jizō Bodhisattva said to remove all thorns from both body and mind of a petitioner. Nowadays most petitioners are senior citizens, come to seek Jizō's aid not for healing but for prevention of senile dementia. Sadly, they often focus on the hope for a sudden death before mental and physical disability can set in.

Contrary to these examples, though, Jizō Bodhisattva is primarily associated with children's illnesses and death. There is a special association of Jizō with miscarried or stillborn infants, or those who die while still in infancy. That association is a frequent cause of the sewing and offering of caps and bibs. What seems an ancient custom but is, in fact, only a few decades old is the practice of offering a Jizō statue to a temple in regret at having aborted a fetus. Japan even now grants only limited access to modern birth control methods, so abortion remains a frequent, sad last resort. It is a matter that not only enriches a medical industry centered on abortion but also enriches many unscrupulous priests who prey on feelings of guilt engendered by an abortion. Offerings to the temples of such priests, they claim, will purify the parents and pacify the spirit of the fetus. Needless to say, Buddhism actually has no such teaching.

16. What are those papers pasted on temples and tied on nearby trees?

It comes as a shock to most Western visitors to see the gates, eaves, columns, and generally every outer area of a venerable temple plastered with bits of paper. Those papers are called *senja fuda,* or votive papers. Each paper has a brief text expressing reverence and the name of the offeror or, more often, offering group. Depending on one's point of view, attaching such a paper to a temple is a mark of respect or is a Japanese version of "Kilroy was here." The placement of papers on the underside of a roof twelve feet or more above the ground or floor has always been something of a mystery to me. I suppose the resident priest of the temple must offer at least passive cooperation in the venture.

Votive papers are most often found on temples that are part of an established pilgrimage route. Usually a group of people making the pilgrimage together will mark their stop at each temple with a votive paper for the group as a body. Temples with long histories and those noted as fortunate places to express one's hopes for the future (otherwise known as praying for some sort of benefit) are also likely to have large collections of votive papers attesting their popularity.

Pilgrimages and temple visits, whether as a group or by oneself, are performed in many ways and for many reasons. The methods range from walking the entire circuit in special pilgrim's garb, sleeping outdoors unless invited into a temple for the night (and leaving early in the morning), begging for food, and offering extensive sutra chanting at each temple, to riding a bus, staying overnight at hot springs resorts, and simply appreciating the noted features of each temple. Reasons may be as religious as marking the death anniversary of a beloved parent, spouse, or child, or may be as secular as having a good time with a congenial group while absorbing something of Japanese culture. Whatever the impetus, a pilgrimage is viewed as a respectful and respected activity.

The thin strips of folded paper tied onto shrubs and trees at a Shinto shrine or Buddhist temple are written oracles, *o-mikuji* in Japanese. These oracles derive from Taoism and commonly use quotations from the Chinese *I-ching* (Book of Changes).The person seeking an oracle shakes a slender stick from a box with a hole in its top just large enough for one stick to emerge. The number on that stick corresponds to one of a large collection of oracles. The shrine or temple attendant locates the proper number and gives a long, thin paper to the seeker. These are not so much "fortunes" of the "You will meet a tall, dark man" variety as they are lists of fortunate and unfortunate days, geographic directions, ages, colors, and so forth. I have often been told that an unlucky oracle should be folded unread and tied to a tree for the Buddha or kami (Shinto guardian spirit) to take care of. This leaves me wondering how one knows that an oracle is unlucky if one has not read it. Perhaps a friend must be brought along for initial evaluation of the results? Other theories include tying an oracle to a tree so that the wind will blow away the ill fortune it predicts and will also spread the good fortune of a prediction. In practice, the oracle receiver seems invariably to read the oracle, perhaps reading aloud to companions, then to fold the paper neatly and tie it to the nearest vacant spot within reach on a bush or tree. In recent years, Meiji Shrine and other large shrines have extended the reach of their o-mikuji by adding English versions for those who can't read the Chinese characters on the standard variety.

17. What does Zen say about creation?

Buddhism has a traditional cosmology, but it is not intended to be taken literally and it does not include any reference to beginning and end, let alone to a purposeful creation.

The basic principles of Buddhism, the criteria by which a teaching can be classified as Buddhist, are:

- Whatever is phenomenal is impermanent
- Whatever is phenomenal is suffering (or unsatisfying)
- Whatever is phenomenal is devoid of self
- Only nirvana is eternally tranquil

Impermanence and having no self-being allow, it seems to me, for neither creation nor creator. Instead of creation, Buddhism speaks of dependent origination, the concept that all phenomena are both the effects of other phenomena and the causes of other phenomena. Phenomenon in this sense includes all of time, space, matter, and energy, as well as all actions. A sheet of paper is a phenomenon. A person writing on that paper is a phenomenon, and both the act of writing and the means used to write are also phenomena. A photon is a phenomenon and so is the universe. The sweetest rose is a phenomenon and so is a reeking trash dump.

The usual explanation given by Buddhists for the endless cycle of cause and effect, of everything being dependent on everything else, is human centered and concerned with religious concepts, but it could be extended to cover physical processes of the physical universe. This Twelve-Linked Chain of Dependent Origination, applied to human concepts, is stated in an early sutra as follows:

> What is dependent origination? On ignorance depend actions. On actions depends consciousness. On consciousness depend name and form. On name and form depend the six sense organs. On the six sense organs depends contact. On contact depends feeling. On feeling depends craving. On craving depends grasping. On grasping depends becoming. On becoming depends birth. On birth depend old age and death, grief, sorrow, suffering, lamentation, and worry. Thus the whole aggregation of suffering arises.
>
> However, if there is no ignorance, actions cease. With the cessation of actions, consciousness ceases. With the cessation of consciousness, name and form cease. With the cessation of name and form, the six sense organs cease. With the cessation of the six sense organs, contact ceases. With the cessation of contact, feeling ceases. With the cessation of feeling, craving ceases. With the cessation of craving, grasping ceases. With the cessation of grasping, becoming ceases. With the cessation of becoming, birth ceases. With the cessation of birth, old age and death, grief, sorrow, suffering, lamentation, and worry cease. Thus the whole aggregation of suffering ceases.

Instead of creation, then, Buddhism teaches us that whatever may arise is brought about by causes and in turn brings about effects.

18. Does Zen have angels?

Heavenly beings are among the categories of existence defined in Buddhist cosmology, and the Japanese term for such beings, *tennin,* is sometimes translated as angel. The heavenly beings, though, have no harps or even wings, and they are not viewed as protecting humans either as individuals or as a class. They simply exist in the heavenly realm, just as we exist in the earthly realm. You may have seen paintings of heavenly maidens soaring across the sky trailing sheer scarves.

There is a famous Japanese legend about one heavenly maiden, the legend of the feather robe, *Hagoromo*. The legend is the basis of a well-known No drama. A heavenly maiden, says the legend, one day was passing over Miho, a sand spit in Suruga Bay. Looking down, she saw sand so white and sparkling that she descended to frolic on the sands. First, though, she hung her feather robe on a pine tree in the grove there. As she danced and played in the clear water and on the sparkling sand, a fisherman happened to enter the pine grove and see her feather robe. What a lovely garment! he thought. Plucking the robe from the tree, the fisherman started to carry it home. Just as he set off, though, he heard a despairing wail. The maiden had returned to don her feather robe so she could fly back to the heavens, but alas the robe had vanished. She was stranded on that beach. The fisherman followed the sound of her cries and soon beheld a creature more wonderful than he ever could have imagined. Despite his distress at her wailing, the entranced fisherman wanted her to remain with him. At last he agreed to return the robe if she would dance for him. So joyously donning the robe that let her fly, the maiden danced first on the white sands and then gradually into the air, rising to her heavenly home.

I first encountered that legend in a novel by Yukio Mishima. Not long afterward, I went to Japan on business and decided one Sunday to see Miho. There is a small enclosure near the edge of a pine grove there, protecting what is said to be the third-generation pine tree growing from the one that held the feathered robe. There is also nearly black sand and dull, polluted-looking water, Suruga Bay being essentially one large harbor for commercial ships of all types. I wonder if the heavenly maiden sometimes looks at it and sighs.

WHAT TITLES AND HONORIFICS
ARE USED FOR ZEN PRIESTS?

1. What terms should I use to address, and to refer to, Buddhist clerics in general and Zen clerics in particular?

The only English titles that are used for Buddhist clerics are reverend and venerable; in general, reverend is used for those affiliated with Japanese Buddhism, and venerable is used for those affiliated with Southeast Asian and Sri Lankan Buddhism. For Chinese, Tibetan, and Korean Buddhism, some use one and some, the other. These titles both are gender neutral. They are always, I think, a respectful and safe choice.

Japanese titles, on the other hand, abound. Most of them are gender neutral, but some are limited to use for female clerics. Some can be applied to anyone in the Buddhist clergy, but others are limited to certain ranks or jobs in the sect organization. Unless you are fully informed as to not only the meaning and Japanese usage of each title but also the usage in the particular group in question, if the group is not Japanese, I recommend that you stick to English and a simple "Reverend Doe" when speaking to the person or "the reverend Marion Doe" when speaking to others about the person.

It is customary in Japan to use a title of some sort in place of a name for both addressing and referring to someone. This applies to everyone (or

at least everyone who is Japanese by ancestry), not just to the clergy. When
speaking to a department manager (in Japanese, *kachō)* named Kaoru
Suzuki, one does not ask "Do you agree, Ms. Suzuki?" let alone "Do you
agree, Kaoru?" The accepted form is "Do you agree, kachō?" One even
asks in the third person, "Has kachō recovered from his cold?" If the conversation includes multiple department managers, when resorting to a
name one also tacks on the title: "Will Suzuki kachō be going to Nagoya?"
is used when the question is directed to Suzuki.

Clerical titles offer considerably greater scope than do mere organiza-
tional assignments and are used even more frequently. One general term
for Buddhist clerics is *oshō.* This can be used for a person holding full
clerical standing (as opposed to trainee standing) in any of the Zen or Pure
Land sects. The same Chinese characters are used in other sects but pronounced *wajō* in the Hossō, Shingon, and Ritsu sects and *kashō* in the
Tendai sects. These terms designated a precepts specialist in early
Buddhism but now are used as a general title of respect.

Another widely used term is *hōjō.* This originally designated the living
quarters of a temple's resident cleric or the area in the center of the ceremony hall that is used only by the officiating cleric. By extension, it has
come to mean the person living in those quarters or officiating in that area.
(The first time someone addressed me as "hōjō-san," I thought she was
talking about the resident priest of the temple rather than about me, the
assistant priest. She asked where "hōjō-san" had been born, and I started to
reply that it was very likely right in the temple's living quarters before I suddenly grasped her meaning and answered "In the United States.")

The term that directly translates to "resident priest" is *jūshoku.* Temple
members (and Buddhist goods salespeople) often ask on the telephone, "Is
jūshoku-san there?" or say, when speaking with the resident priest,
"Jūshoku-san has always been so kind to our family."

Less-elevated forms include *o-bō-san,* which can be applied to both
males and females but usually is used only for males, and *anju-san,* which
is used exclusively for females. Though properly limited to full clerics
(both derive from terms for a resident priest), these terms are often used
for trainees as well.

Among the more specialized terms are *sensei,* rōshi, and zenji. Because
these are so commonly used (and commonly *mis*used) in Western groups,
each is addressed in its own separate question.

2. What does sensei mean, and who can be called a sensei?

The term sensei literally means one who has lived before, the implication being that there must have been at least one previous life for the person to accumulate so much wisdom and virtue. Sensei is used most often for teachers of anything at any level. A college professor is sensei, and so is a kindergarten teacher. A high-ranked teacher of the tea ceremony or another traditional art is sensei. Medical doctors and dentists are always sensei. Clergy members are sensei when one doesn't wish to bother with something fancier. And politicians are sensei, without even a hint of sarcasm.

Although oshō, hōjō, jūshoku, and anju usually are suffixed with a general term of courtesy, *san* or *sama,* when used in place of a name (e.g., hōjō-san, oshō-sama), sensei substitutes for san or sama and does not, by itself, take a suffix.

3. Who is a rōshi in Sōtōshū?

The term rōshi, literally "old teacher" or "old master," is used quite differently according to the sect of the cleric to whom it applies. In Sōtōshū, it is simply a term of respect with no special meaning attached. Any Sōtōshū cleric past the trainee stage may properly be addressed or referred to as "rōshi."

In Sōtōshū, rōshi is a convenient term for any cleric whose other titles escape one's mind at the moment. It is, perhaps, most widely used as a part of the polite language applied to one's partner in dialog and, by extension, to all persons associated with the dialog partner. For example, when I talk with you, I refer to my master (the priest to whom I apprenticed) simply as "shishō," which means "the person to whom I am apprenticed," whether the apprenticeship is in the clergy or carpentry. *Your* (priest) master, on the other hand, becomes "rōshi."

Another frequent use of "rōshi" in Sōtōshū is in mailing addresses. The first time I received a card addressed to me as "rōshi" rather than the conventional, all-purpose "sama," I thought the sender—my master—must be put out with me about something. When I asked, he laughed and said it was just that one of his assistants at Eiheiji had helped address the several hundred New Year's greeting cards he had to send; the cards were divided into those to clergy and those to laity, and all those to clergy were addressed with rōshi instead of sama. That system is so widely used that nowadays I don't even notice whether I m addressed as sama or as rōshi.

4. Who is a rōshi in Rinzaishū or Ōbakushū?

In Rinzaishū and Ōbakushū, rōshi is a defined rank of the clergy. The person holding that rank must have completed the training course required in the particular sect (Rinzaishū consists of about fifteen independent sects in Japan). This usually means satisfactory completion of a long koan series under an established rōshi. (In the Myōshinji Rinzai sect, for example, the series totals more than one thousand.) It is not necessary to achieve rōshi ranking in order to become resident priest of a temple, but only a rōshi can conduct koan training or become chief priest of a head temple. It is said that only one or two of the hundreds of Rinzai clerics in training at any given time will ever reach the standing of rōshi. For those who do, the average time required is on the order of one to two decades, most of which must be spent in a head temple as either priest-trainee or temple officer. This, then, is a far different usage than Sōtōshū's casual courtesy title.

5. Who is a rōshi in Sanbōkyōdan?

The special case of Sanbōkyōdan is interesting because of its pervasive influence within the United States.

Sanbōkyōdan is a very small organization that has exerted a remarkably large influence on Zen in the United States. It was founded in 1954 by Reverend Hakuun Yasutani, originally a Sōtōshū priest, whose dharma lineage included priests trained in Rinzaishū temples. The distinguishing characteristics of Sanbōkyōdan are a single-minded pursuit of the kenshō experience, as defined by that organization, and its establishment of teachers who are not clerics. It is a religious movement of, and for, laypeople. The influence outside Japan resulted from the fact that many Westerners, including a number of European Catholic monastics, practiced under Rev. Yasutani. Those who trained under Rev. Yasutani include the noted lay teachers Philip Kapleau and Robert Aitken, as well as the Reverend Eidō Shimano, and the Reverend Hakuyū Taizan Maezumi, all of whom founded Zen centers in the United States.

Within Sanbōkyōdan, the terms "sensei" and "rōshi" have specific meanings and are in no way interchangeable. To be called "sensei," a

Sanbōkyōdan member must be certified as experiencing kenshō then must complete a curriculum of six or seven hundred koans (which set, however, is covered at a rapid pace and can usually be completed in about five years), receiving a piece of calligraphy as evidence of authorization to lead others in Zen practice. To be called "rōshi," the Sanbōkyōdan sensei must demonstrate maturity in Zen practice until the supervising rōshi grants a teaching name and holds a public ceremony of acknowledgment, and must be promoted to "provisional teacher" rank. The final rank of "teacher" maintains the title of rōshi and confers the authority to validate kenshō.

Because this Sanbōkyōdan system is so different from the usage of the same terms in the older Zen sects, Zen clerics from those sects usually are nonplussed when asked by an American, "Are you a sensei or a rōshi?"

6. Who is a Zen master?

The Japanese term zenji is written with Chinese characters meaning Zen and master, or teacher. One might expect, then, that the English term "Zen master" and the Japanese term "zenji" have the same meaning. This is not, however, the case. The English term Zen master, and its Western-language cognates, has no real synonym in Japanese. I am often asked, "Is so-and-so a Zen master?" (Less often, "Are you a Zen master?") I'm never sure what to reply. I can only guess that a Zen master is a priest who has at least one apprentice.

Based on the derivation of the term, it seems that an apprentice cleric in a Zen sect would use "zenji" for that apprentice's master. That is not so, however. One's own master is "shishō" (whether the apprenticeship is to a Zen cleric or a tea ceremony teacher or a plumber) or, more specifically, "shisō," in which the "sō" designates a cleric.

Zenji has, in the course of Japanese history, been a designation for a specialist in meditation (as distinguished, for example, from a specialist in precepts), an honorary title awarded by the emperor to an outstanding cleric of any sect, a generalized title for clerics in a Zen sect, and a title of respect for the chief priest of a head temple in one of the Zen sects.

Only the last usage remains for contemporary figures in Sōtōshū. Only a person who is, or has been, chief priest of Eiheiji or Sōjiji, Sōtōshū's two head temples, is referred to (and addressed) as zenji. When the identity of the person is clear, it is common to say "Zenji-sama" whether addressing the zenji directly or referring to the zenji in conversation with another person.

Usage of zenji differs between Sōtō and Rinzai sects in a mirror image of the differing usage of rōshi. In Rinzaishū, any priest whose rank is sufficient for becoming resident priest of a temple may be called zenji. The term seems, however, to be seldom used in Rinzaishū.

7. What about dōchō and kanchō?

Dōchō is a term used primarily for the head of a training temple for priests, although it can be used as a term of respect for the resident priest of any temple. The two Chinese characters for this word are "hall" or "building" and "head." So the dōchō is the head of the training hall. Another character with the same chō pronunciation is used in most terms meaning the head of an organization: *kaichō* for the president or chairperson of an organization, *shachō* for the president of a corporation, *gakuchō* for a school principal, and many others.

Kanchō is a term used in Japanese law until the 1860s to designate the highest-ranked priest of each recognized religious sect. It is still used in that meaning by most sects. Within the Zen group, there is a kanchō of the Ōbaku sect, one of each of the Rinzai sects (Myōshinji, Kenchōji, Engakuji, Nanzenji, etc.), and one of the Sōtō sect, that office being alternately held by the chief priests of Sōtōshū's two head temples.

WHAT CHARACTERIZES JAPANESE BUDDHISM OVERALL AND ZEN BUDDHISM IN PARTICULAR?

1. What is Zen?

Zen is a perfume; a sports star; a Tokyo restaurant; a footed tray or low table on which traditional Japanese meals are served; the Japanese word for all or, when doubled *(zenzen)* for never, not at all; and an American term for obscure language or idiosyncratic actions.

It is, more pertinently, the Japanese pronunciation of a Chinese character pronounced "ch'an," which was used for transliteration into written Chinese of the first syllable of the Sanskrit *dhyana,* meaning a concentrated mind or meditation in which opposites become one. Such a concentrated mind certainly is one aspect of original Buddhism. Several Buddhist texts, such as the Mahavagga, detail the story of Shakyamuni Buddha's awakening that occurred when he sat with concentrated mind beneath a tree at Bodhgaya.

Special focus on concentrated mind is said to have been transmitted from India to China by Bodhidharma, cited in Zen teachings as twenty-eighth in the Indian dharma lineage starting with Shakyamuni Buddha's disciple Mahakashyapa and as the first in the subsequent Chinese dharma lineage. It is said that one day when Shakyamuni Buddha was to address his followers, instead of speaking he silently held up a lotus flower. Seeing the flower, Mahakashyapa smiled in understanding, thus becoming the first person to receive the dharma without words. Bodhidharma is thought to have traveled by ship from India to southern China. In an episode that is widely cited in Zen literature, he soon went to visit Emperor Wu, of the Liang dynasty, at the southern capital. Emperor Wu told the Indian priest about the Buddhist temples he had built and the support he had provided to China's Buddhist clerics, then asked what merit he had accumulated through these efforts. Bodhidharma answered, "No merit." The emperor then asked what is the essential meaning of the sacred dharma. The answer he received was, "In the infinity of space there is nothing sacred." Completely baffled, the emperor finally asked, "Who *is* this person standing before me?" To which Bodhidharma responded, "Unknown."

Unsurprisingly, Bodhidharma left the capital shortly after that interview. He settled in a cave in northern China, at the site of Shaolin temple, and sat motionless in zazen for nine years. For this reason, the Daruma (the Japanese nickname for Bodhidharma) dolls popular in Japan have no legs, merely a rounded base so that no matter how the doll is tilted, it returns to the upright position.

The Indian dhyana teachings gradually became combined with Taoist elements in China, yielding the Ch'an school of Buddhism. The Ch'an teachings were later transmitted to Japan by a number of Japanese and Chinese priests, first as a part of early Japanese Buddhism and of the Tendai sect, then as the Sōtō, Rinzai, and Ōbaku Zen sects.

When the word *Zen* is used in this book, it means the religion of Japan's Sōtōshū, Rinzaishū (in all its branches), and Ōbakushū, and that of direct offshoots of those three sects in other parts of the world.

2. What are the differences among sects within Japanese Zen?

There are three major types of Zen Buddhism: Sōtōshū, Rinzaishū, and Ōbakushū. Within Rinzaishū, there are a number of different sects. All three types were brought to Japan from China, but it was in Japan that they first were established as individual sects that are organizationally separate from each other. Rinzaishū was the first to reach Japan and the only one that has multiple founders in Japan. Sōtōshū, which followed quickly on the heels of Rinzaishū, was brought to Japan by Dōgen, a Japanese priest who had gone to China and trained under a priest in the Ts'ao-tung (in Japanese pronunciation, Sōtō) lineage, and returned to Japan in 1227. Ōbakushū was founded in Japan by a Chinese priest, Yin-yuan Lung-ch'i (in Japanese pronunciation, Ingen Ryūki), who reached Japan in 1654 and was given a Chinese Ming-style temple near Kyoto in 1661. Although Ōbakushū has never been a large sect, Ingen's teachings did much to reinvigorate the Sōtō and Rinzai sects established some four hundred years earlier.

It is often said that Rinzaishū is the Zen of the nobility and Sōtōshū is that of the common people. Certainly Rinzaishū has been the leader in the blending of Zen and Japanese arts, such as tea ceremony, flower arranging, calligraphy, and poetry, and in the interplay of Zen and martial arts. Until recent times, such matters were practiced only by the nobility and high-ranking commoners.

The main reason for that saying, though, is probably the use of koan practice in Rinzaishū and of "just sitting" in Sōtōshū. The classical study of a koan series requires a classical education for elucidation of the koans. The level of language proficiency (the number of thousands of Chinese characters known), and the breadth of background in Buddhism and in both Chinese and Japanese culture, were until recently out of reach of most Japanese. "Just sitting," on the other hand, is a practice that relies primarily on action (or rather, *in*action) combined with listening to the explanations of priests. The educational demands and time required for "just sitting" are thus much more modest than those for koan practice.

Ōbakushū stems from a Chinese Rinzai lineage, so it also emphasizes koan practice. In the three- to four-hundred-year interval between the arrivals of other Rinzaishū lineages and the founding of Ōbakushū, however, Chinese Buddhism had undergone changes. The dominant varieties of Buddhism were reduced to two: the esoteric Buddhism of Tibet and Mongolia, and a blending of Zen and Pure Land Buddhism. (These are still the dominant varieties of Buddhism in China, with esoteric Buddhism mostly in the northwest and the exoteric Zen–Pure Land blend in the rest of the Buddhist areas.) It was the latter combined Buddhism that was transmitted by Ōbakushū. Modern Ōbakushū uses the invocation of Amida Buddha's name (nembutsu) in addition to zazen.

3. What are the differences between the Zen sects and the rest of Japanese Buddhism?

The annual religious survey published by the Japanese government divides established Buddhism into six groups of sects that are listed in the approximate order of their founding, except that the very first Japanese Buddhism is represented by the last group. In order of origin, then, the six groupings are Nara Buddhism, having roots in Japan's earliest Buddhism in the sixth century, but properly speaking started in the seventh century; Tendai-related, stemming from Saichō's return from China in 805; Shingon-related, starting with Kūkai's return from China in 806; Pure Land–related, begun by Hōnen in 1175; Zen-related, with founding dates starting as early as 1191; and Nichiren-related, founded by Nichiren in 1253. Just as the dates of origination fall into three periods, many of the characteristics of the groups of sects reflect the influences of those three periods. The Zen sects fit in the middle position within the last period of the origins of established Buddhism.

All of Japanese Buddhism falls within the Mahayana tradition, a movement that began in India within Buddhism's first five centuries. Today's southern Asian Buddhism is mostly in the Theravada tradition, a conservative tradition that accepts only the early group of scriptures. Mahayana, in contrast, accepts later writings and practices, and is the Buddhism of northern and eastern Asia.

The sects from Japan's Nara period, from about 646 to 794, were not initially "sects" as we use the term today. Like their Chinese models, several priests specialized in the study and practice of particular sutras, and the temples of those priests came to be known for the sutras taught there. Buddhism in this period still was a matter for the imperial court and its nobles, with very little involvement of common people. (This, too, was a reflection of Chinese models.) The primary duty of priests was considered to be rituals and chanting dedicated to the well-being of the nation, as embodied in its court. That individual priests often took issue with that objective is shown by the long series of imperial edicts forbidding priests to leave their temples and go among the common people. (Needless to say, today's Nara sects are as much devoted to the religious concerns of ordinary people as are other modern sects.)

The Chinese Tendai teachings brought to Japan by Saichō were an integrative effort, showing the interrelationships among major Mahayana sutras and posing the Lotus Sutra at the peak. Saichō and his successor Ennin increased the integrative movement, studying Zen, Pure Land, and esoteric practices in China and incorporating those practices in the Tendai center at Mount Hiei, outside Kyoto. Like the Nara temples, Tendai was supported by the imperial court and primarily served that court. Among

Tendai's great accomplishments was the loosening of control over religion by the court, however. Just after the death of Saichō, Tendai was allowed to establish its own precepts platform. Before that only one precepts platform existed, in Nara, and candidates for the priesthood had to be approved by the court then assigned by the court to one of the Nara temples. With its separate precepts platform, Tendai became able to confer a different set of precepts (called the "bodhisattva precepts") that omits most of the detailed regulations of the earlier precepts. Priesthood candidates could receive the Tendai precepts at Mount Hiei, then be registered with the court during the period of their studies and training within the Mount Hiei complex.

Although several esoteric practices are included in Tendai Buddhism, it is the Shingon teachings brought by Kūkai that are the main embodiment of esoteric Buddhism. Today esoteric Buddhism outside Japan is represented mainly by Tibetan and Mongolian traditions. Shingon Buddhism focuses primarily on words and actions that can be properly understood only by priests who have undergone extensive training and initiations. Outward indications of esoteric practices, present within both Shingon and Tendai branches of Japanese Buddhism, include the creation and use of mandalas (symbolic designs representing the universe) and the chanting of dharanis (incantations preserving the original Sanskrit words).

Almost four centuries after the establishment of Japan's Tendai and Shingon sects, a series of Tendai priests broke away to found their own movements based on single elements of the integrated Tendai tradition. Within a little over a century, Japan saw the creation of four branches of Pure Land, two branches of Zen, and two branches of Nichiren Buddhism. All of these were based on single practices that could be understood and performed by lay adherents among the common people. All asserted greater independence from the courts (imperial and shogunal) and nobility, reaching beyond the limited urban centers to spread Buddhist teachings throughout the nation.

Hōnen received the precepts on Mount Hiei at the age of fourteen. He soon entered a temple within the Hiei complex that focused primarily on the practice of nembutsu, repeated invocations of Amida Buddha, one of Buddhism's many figures representing the power of compassion. At the age of forty-three, he resolved his inner questions and set off for Kyoto, determined to carry the practice of nembutsu to all people. Simple repetition of the one phrase, *Namu Amida Butsu* (Praise to Amida Buddha), he thought, was the one Buddhist practice demanding no wealth, no protracted learning, no freedom to devote one's time solely to religion. Anyone could practice nembutsu even while laboring in a rice paddy. Hōnen's support of nembutsu as the sole practice for Buddhists was vigorously opposed by many Tendai priests, even while his profound learning was applauded by others. Hōnen's Pure Land (Jōdo) teachings were extended by one of his followers, Shinran, who founded the True Pure Land (Jōdo Shin) branch. The combined membership of the two present sects of Jōdo Shin makes this the largest of Japan's established Buddhist groups.

Another Tendai priest, Eisai, brought contemporary Zen teachings and practice from China to Japan. Although earlier Zen thought had been known in Japan, it was limited primarily to the priesthood. Eisai started the process of spreading Zen to laypeople. His example was followed by a number of Japanese and Chinese priests who established temples, which became sects, in the Rinzai Zen tradition, and by Dōgen, who worked to promulgate the Sōtō Zen tradition. Dōgen's followers broke away from the custom of relying on the court and nobility for temple financing, and instead appealed to lower-ranking supporters. The practices of zazen and koans were promoted by the Zen sects as the sole necessary Buddhist practice, much in the way that Pure Land sects promoted nembutsu practice.

The third breakaway from Tendai teachings was Nichiren, who acclaimed the Lotus Sutra as the ultimate Buddhist teaching, abrogating the need for other sutras or practices. Common people could simply invoke the power of the Lotus Sutra by chanting *Namu Myōhōrengekyō* (Praise to the Lotus Sutra). Nichiren and his followers spread throughout Japan to carry that message to everyone, just as the Pure Land and Zen priests had widely promulgated their own one-practice teachings. Nichiren-related lay organizations are dominant in today's Buddhist "new religions" (founded in the nineteenth century or later).

Zen, then, shares with the Pure Land and Nichiren groups a focus on religion for common people through a single main practice. It is distinguished from the other two groups by having the common practice of zazen and koan study, rather than the practice of chanting an invocation.

4. How is Buddhism different from Christianity?

The first time I was faced with this question was after a lecture for Tokyo's Buddhist English Academy. The pan-Buddhist organization was founded to assist both priests and laypeople in explaining Buddhism in English. My talk had centered on the concept of Christian monasticism and its inapplicability to Buddhism. After a lively question period, the chairwoman announced that two minutes were available for a last quick question, and this was the question raised! I answered that a whole series of lectures would be needed for even a cursory reply. Now I feel an entire bookcase would be needed. Nonetheless I'll try to mention a few overall differences. Each of the contrasts below is true only for some of the many varieties of Buddhism and of Christianity. They are, however, typical of the total ranges covered by these two world religions.

The basic difference, I think, is not theism or nontheism but rather is the focus on life in the present versus a life after death. Shakyamuni Buddha was asked about existence after the death of a human and about the existence of (gender-neutral) gods. He replied that although his awakening allowed him to see the answers to such questions, the answers would not help anyone in the vital matter of living this present life. He therefore declined to discuss those matters. Instead, the Buddha presented guidance for living each moment with open eyes.

One of the results of the focus on the present is that Buddhism's teachings are valid regardless of the historicity of Shakyamuni Buddha. We accept the teachings because people have affirmed their truth for more than two and a half millennia.

Another major difference is the Buddhist view of humans as inherently good beings, capable of awakening, despite the evil they may create through ignorance. The evil that occurs brings more evil, as the good brings more good. Christianity views evil as a sin, an offense against God, and views humans as inherently sinful beings in need of divine forgiveness to escape eternal suffering.

These, then, are the broad themes pervading the two religions. Both have multitudes of variations founded in geography and history, but each has usually retained these characteristics. The greatest shared characteristic is an attempt to understand the workings of all existence and to replace suffering and hatred with peace and love among all beings.

5. Isn't all Japanese religion Zen?

In a word, no. Zen is one branch of Buddhism, and Buddhism is one branch of Japanese religion. Indigenous religion became organized and less localized following the transmission of organized Buddhism and Taoism to Japan from China and Korea. The result eventually became known as Shinto, the way of the spirits, and Shugendō, the way of mountain ascetics. Over the centuries, additional religions (notably Confucian-ism) arrived in Japan. With the exception of Christianity, which demanded exclusive allegiance of its believers, all the varieties of religion were observed by most people, and little differentiation was made by laypeople or even by priests.

Government support and control of religion became stricter in the early seventeenth century. In 1589, Japan outlawed Christianity—a ban that endured more than 300 years—and later instituted a requirement that each family be registered in a Buddhist temple. The temple priests were required to maintain membership registers of each family and to certify that no member families observed Christian practices or possessed Christian symbols. The certification requirement gave birth to a custom that continues, in part, even today: at the time of the summer Obon ceremonies, priests visit the homes of member families and chant sutras dedicated to the members who have died. Originally, these visits included inspections of the home altar for evidence of Christian worship.

Official and unofficial melding of all religious branches, creating in effect a single entity of "Japanese religion," was abruptly terminated by law in the 1870s. The new government under the emperor, free of the shoguns' power, worked to promote Shinto and to repress Buddhism. Religious centers that formerly included both Buddhist and Shinto facilities were forcibly divided. Clergies of the two were separated. Shugendō practice areas were required to affiliate with Shinto or (less commonly) Buddhist organizations.

Despite all this effort toward religious separation, today's Japanese families usually maintain both Shinto and Buddhist ties. In a well-known phrase, they are "born and married Shinto, but die Buddhist." Clerics who are priests in both religions still are not uncommon. In my own Sōtō sect, I know of one major mountain temple, certified as a training temple for new priests, that maintains rituals of clearly Shinto origin. Another Sōtōshū temple in central Tokyo is also a major shrine to Inari, the Shinto spirit of the rice plant.

Urbanization seems to be gradually reducing Buddhist activities and Shinto activities as well. Perhaps modern population shift will eventually accomplish what government edict attempted but could not enforce.

6. Is Zen a religion? Is Buddhism a religion?

One classic definition of religion states that religion concerns the relationship between humans and one or more goddesses or gods. By that definition, Buddhism is not a religion. In modern thought, however, theism is not a necessary characteristic of a religion. Modern scholars generally say instead that the performance of religious acts constitutes the existence of a religion. Under this definition, Buddhism is most certainly a religion and so is the branch of Buddhism called Zen.

Actions by ordinary Japanese reveal an interesting range of institutions viewed as religious, although the people performing those actions probably consider themselves to be "nonreligious." Passing in front of a Buddhist temple or Shinto shrine, or even a single statue of, for example, Jizō Bodhisattva or the foxes representing the Shinto rice spirit Inari, Japanese in overwhelming number pause to signal respect by raising hands in Buddhist reverence and bowing, or by clapping raised hands twice to summon the Shinto kami (spirit), or most probably by combining the two actions. At one of the (relatively few) Confucian temples, the same acts are performed but by fewer people. Christian churches and religious centers of other religions rarely are accorded this passing salute.

The terms "religion" and "religious" are comparatively recent additions to the Japanese language. Both use a pair of Chinese characters specifically devised to translate the English word "religion" and its European-language cognates into Japanese. One scholar of religion has reported that many Japanese associate the word "religion" with middle-aged women who come to the door on Sunday and ask embarrassing questions! This may answer the puzzle of people who state that they have no religion even though they attend religious weddings, funerals, memorial services, and other observances for themselves, their families, and their friends, in addition to paying respects to religious institutions and images both when merely passing by and when making special visits.

7. What god do Zen Buddhists worship?

Buddhism is not, properly speaking, a theistic religion. The historical Buddha, Shakyamuni, was a completely human being who understood profound truths about all beings and our universe, then showed others the way to understand those truths. The other buddhas—Amida Buddha,

Mahavairochana Buddha, Maitreya Buddha, and others—are not gods but rather idealized beings.

It is human, though, to want some powerful being to help us when we have trouble. This is especially true when we don't understand the cause of the trouble and how to remedy it. It was not so long, therefore, before Buddhists started to rely on the power of compassion, especially, as conveyed by the figures of Amida Buddha, Kannon Bodhisattva, Jizō Bodhisattva, and others. Along with that reliance came the concept of Buddhist merit.

One of the main principles of Buddhism is that acting so as to help and benefit other people, and other beings of all sorts, leads the way toward a universe of kindness. Acts in accordance with that principle are considered meritorious acts. They are not considered to be acts that will please some buddha or bodhisattva, nor are they considered to be acts that will directly benefit ourselves.

Among the possible meritorious acts, even in the earliest times, were providing food to the Buddhist home leavers and sheltering them during India's rainy season. The first Buddhists included four categories: male and female home leavers, and male and female householders. The former, like Shakyamuni Buddha himself, left home and family to roam the country teaching others about Buddhism through both speech and actions. One cannot ceaselessly roam while raising food crops, so one of the roles of the householders, who practiced Buddhism within their homes and families, was to provide food to the home leavers. Although home leavers roamed about for nine months of the year, it was not practical to do so during the three-month rainy season. During that period, home leavers gathered to recite the sutras together and refresh their memories, to lessen the spread of divergent versions. It was a good opportunity to educate new home leavers in the Buddhist teachings. Householders also could listen to the recitations, memorize sutras, and learn about Buddhism. The householders provided shelters for home leavers so that gatherings could occur.

After a while, though, these selfless acts on the part of householders came to be viewed as a sort of point system; the more points one accumulated, the better one's life would be. Needless to say, that is not at all the proper Buddhist concept, but it suits the minds of people who are not yet fully awakened to reality.

It is not surprising, then, that modern Buddhists faced with troubles will often offer "meritorious acts" dedicated to Buddhist beings whose

158 | help they wish to receive. This is certainly close to the concept of "worshiping a god" but is not a part of the formal Buddhist teachings.

8. Why is Zen so authoritarian and hierarchical?

Zen, in my own experience, rarely succeeds in being authoritarian, although some people try to make it so, and is hierarchical mostly in name and very little in fact.

This was brought home to me when Sōtōshū issued a revised book of dedications for use in sutra readings. I was curious to see what changes had been made, so I bought a copy. The dedications being used at Taisōji at that time were from a book several editions earlier, which considerably predated the edition I had used before becoming Taisōji's assistant priest. Liking the revised version, I asked the resident priest whether I might use the dedications from that book. Perhaps that might be viewed as an authoritarian system, but I saw it as simple courtesy inasmuch as he was (and is) responsible for all Taisōji activities. What is notable to me is that Sōtōshū made no attempt to require its temples to use the revised version. Clearly that absence of pressure applied not only to the one revision in question but also to a whole series of past revisions. We continued for some years with the new dedications when I was reading them and the old dedications when the resident priest was reading them.

A young Sōtōshū priest I encountered told me a story about one of the sect's chief priests. Soon after his installation as Eiheiji's *kanshū*, the new leader decided that brown, rather than white, rice should be served in Eiheiji for reasons of nutrition. The young priest, an Eiheiji trainee at the time, said that this seemingly simple change caused months of negotiations, ending in a compromise that allocated brown rice to the priest-trainees and white rice to everyone else except, I assume, the kanshū himself.

Zen temples affiliated with Sōtōshū or one of the Rinzai sects do have positions in a hierarchy that descends from the head temple of the sect through temples historically connected and finally reaches the individual temple, which may have other temples below it as well. There are formal requirements that consent of the resident priest of the temple one level up must be obtained for certain actions. I heard of two temples, however, that were located near each other and quite a distance from their respective higher-level temples. Instead of going to the distant higher-level temples, the resident priests of the two nearby temples simply stamped consent on each other's papers.

In a word, no. The Buddhist precept about not killing has been interpreted in some times and some places as banning the eating of meat, with various interpretations placed on what constitutes "meat." This is by no means universal, however. The ban on meat eating has always been primarily directed at the Buddhist clergy, and it has been mostly limited to the area of China and Korea.

Theravada Buddhism, the main form of Buddhism in Southeast Asia and in Sri Lanka, does not forbid meat. Buddhist clerics in Theravada are required to obtain their food by daily begging rounds and to eat solid food only before noon. Meat, whether that of a mammal or that of fish or poultry, can be offered to a cleric in the begging bowl and can be eaten by the cleric if three conditions are met:

- the cleric did not kill the animal
- the cleric did not ask anyone to kill the animal
- the cleric has no reason to believe that the animal was killed specifically for a food offering.

The observance of the three conditions, rather than a ban on meat, is what has been followed in Japan.

Japan has few indigenous meat animals, but fish and, to a lesser extent, fowl have been a part of the Japanese diet from early times. Fish and shellfish remains characterize the sites of habitations that predate rice cultivation in Japan. When Buddhism entered Japan from China and Korea, the strictures concerning meat were not applied to seafood.

A story concerning Shinran, the founder of Jōdo Shinshū, illustrates views in the early thirteenth century. Shinran was once among the group of clerics invited to the home of a nobleman to proofread a copy the noble had made of the Buddhist canon. During the proofreading sessions the priests wore their full clerical costume of kimono, over-robe, and buddha robe. At mealtimes, they removed the outermost buddha robe so as to feel free to enjoy fish and fowl. Shinran, however, kept his buddha robe on while he ate some fish. The noble's son asked him persistently why he alone kept on the buddha robe, not accepting Shinran's first answer that he had just forgotten to remove it. Finally Shinran explained that although he believed there were, in that age, no precepts to be followed, by wearing the symbol of a Buddhist follower he hoped to convey some religious benefit to the fish.

The dietary emphasis in Japanese Buddhism is on appreciating the food that enables us to continue our lives. Whether animal or plant, our food was once alive. By consuming all food with care and thankfulness, we respect the life of that food.

I once was invited to take part in a luncheon following a memorial service for the hostess's late husband. It was held in a restaurant specializing in a kind of Zen vegetarian cuisine originated by Ōbakushū. Each dish was prepared with the closest attention not only to taste but also to appearance and presentation. I was so rapt in enjoyment of this rare treat that I was not listening to a discussion between the restaurant owner and one of the hostess's sons-in-law. When the owner directly appealed to me for endorsement of his statements, though, I had to pause and pay attention. The son-in-law had hardly touched any of his food. When asked why he was not eating, he replied that he found such fare tasteless and preferred a diet featuring red meat. The restaurant owner then told him that even the pickled Japanese apricot had once had a life, growing on a tree in the sun and fresh air. A farm family had devoted their lives to helping apricots to grow on the trees and later to harvesting the fruit. Other people took great care to convey the fruit to market without bruising its delicate flesh. Finally the restaurant owner had gone to the early morning produce market to select the very best apricots. Cooks at the restaurant pickled the apricots in a process that demanded their attention for more than a week. The cooks and servers then presented the beautiful and delicious result to us. By eating the apricots with sincere appreciation, we brought them into a new form of life, as part of our bodies. The son-in-law, on the other hand, was terminating the life of the apricot and denigrating the lives of all the people who had participated in bringing it to him. This was a view in which I heartily concurred. Then I brought the spurned apricot to new life by eating it myself. Truly delicious!

10. What precepts must Zen priests observe?

Japan's Buddhism in general places little emphasis on Buddhist precepts. The large sets of specific rules of conduct for clerics that are followed in Korean, Chinese, and southern Asian Buddhism are not incorporated in Japan's practice. All that remains in Japan are the precepts themselves, a much smaller set of principles. Some Japanese Buddhist sects, indeed, have done away with precepts altogether.

In the Zen sects, a new apprentice receives sixteen precepts, promising to live by the guidance of those precepts. The sixteen include three groups: the Three Refuges, Three Pure Precepts, and Ten Grave Prohibitions.

The first group is thought to have been used since the time of Shakyamuni Buddha. It consists of the following statements:

I take refuge in the Buddha (or, my life is founded in the
 Buddha).
I take refuge in the dharma—the Buddhist teachings (or, my
 life is founded in the dharma).
I take refuge in the sangha—those who follow the Buddha (or,
 my life is founded in the sangha).

The second group, the Three Pure Precepts, state Buddhist principles in the broadest terms:

Refrain from what promotes evil.
Do what promotes good.
Act so as to benefit others.

The Ten Grave Prohibitions follow as more specific methods of following the pure precepts. These precepts consist of refraining from three kinds of actions, four kinds of words, and three kinds of thoughts. They are as follows:

Not to kill
Not to steal
Not to engage in wrongful sexual activity
Not to lie
Not to encourage use of intoxicants
Not to speak ill of others
Not to praise oneself, and not to be too proud to praise others
Not to covet either dharma or property
Not to give way to anger
Not to disparage the "three treasures"—the Buddha, dharma,
 and sangha

There is a story about a Chinese priest who lived in a tree and was therefore called Zen Master Bird's Nest. A famous general came to visit him and asked, "What is the most important Buddhist teaching?" Zen Master Bird's Nest replied, "It is: Refrain from what promotes evil; do what promotes good; act so as to benefit others." The general had expected some wonderfully metaphysical phrase that would be difficult to comprehend. He complained, "Even a child of three knows that!" And the answer was, "Yes, even a child of three knows that, but a person of eighty still has difficulty in practicing it."

Buddhism teaches that "evil" and "good," like all our human concepts, exist only in relation to each other. We can say that act A is evil only by observing that it is not good. And conversely, we can say that act B is good only because we judge it to be not evil. No phenomenon can be purely evil or purely good, because no one phenomenon can exist independently of all other phenomena. So when we seek to refrain from what promotes evil, we also in some measure refrain from what promotes good. When we seek to promote good, we also in some measure promote evil. Acts performed to benefit ourselves may benefit others as well, and acts performed to benefit others according to our imperfect human understanding often actually benefit ourselves and work against the benefit of others. No act is pure, independent cause. All acts are effects of all the phenomena of the whole universe and all of time; all acts are causes of all the phenomena of the whole universe and all of time. Thus the Three Pure Precepts, though they sound elementary and simple, are actually impossible to accomplish. We can only try our best to hold these precepts as a beacon showing a path we can walk.

Similarly the Ten Grave Prohibitions cannot be perfected in our human lives. We vow to live without killing. But no one can live without taking the lives of many other beings. Not only people have lives; animals, birds, fish, insects, microbes, plants, and all the other forms of being have lives. We must eat to sustain our human lives. The most we can do, then, is to respect the lives of all the forms of being that make up our food. If we accept the nutrition necessary to continue life, treating all the foods we use with care and appreciation, those foods become a part of another life: our own. If we thoughtlessly waste the foods that could support other lives, those foods have been ruthlessly killed.

We vow to live without telling lies. Yet the truth of reality cannot be captured in words. Thus the very act of speaking creates an element of untruth. Beyond that, we must consider which truth we speak. Visiting a family member in the hospital, if we state accurately that "You look as though you may die any instant," the message conveyed is that we hate that family member and are hoping for an early death. Presumably in such a case, we would not bother visiting the hospital, so the message received by the patient is a lie. Conversely, if we say, "You look as though you have made a good start on recovery already!" it may not be an accurate recital of our impressions, but the message received by the patient will be the truth that we love that person and are hoping for a speedy and complete recovery. For someone who has taken the trouble to visit, that can be assumed to be a truth. Every word has far-reaching meanings, and no word can be completely true.

When we seek not to encourage the use of intoxicants, normally we think only of such intoxicants as alcohol or drugs. Yet the most intoxicating, and the most dangerous, is not a physical substance but words.

In vowing to follow the precepts, we must carefully consider that total adherence to the stated precepts is incompatible with human life. These are not human laws, nor are they things that the Buddha has ordered us to obey. They are guidelines to the direction we try to follow in order that our lives may enrich the universe.

11. What precepts must Zen laypeople observe?

The Zen precepts that are given to laypeople who wish to become formal lay Buddhists are exactly the same as the precepts given to people who wish to become Buddhist priests.

Let us first consider why only the precepts *(shila)* are used for priests and not the rules of conduct *(vinaya)*. Also, we can consider why the Zen sects rarely mention the precepts.

When Buddhism first came to Japan from China and Korea, the Chinese system of government control of Buddhism soon followed. Rather than independent sects, there were temples that specialized in one form of Buddhist teachings or in one sutra. The government controlled the number of apprentices who could enter training each year and how many of those apprentices would be sent to which temple. Part of the mechanism for control was the government establishment of precepts platforms (only one at first) where the new clerics could receive both precepts and rules of conduct. The founder of Japan's Tendaishū, Saichō, felt strongly that the training of Buddhist priests should be a matter controlled by Buddhist priests, not court officials. To this end, he campaigned for permission to establish his own precepts platform at Mount Hiei, the

Tendaishū main temple complex outside Kyoto. Although Saichō was unsuccessful in this to the end of his life, not long after his death the government relented and gave permission for the separate precepts platform. Based on Saichō's teachings, which in turn were based on Chinese T'ient'ai teachings, the only precepts given at the Tendaishū platform were the bodhisattva precepts. These included the Ten Good Precepts and Ten Grave Prohibitions, which are basically the positive and negative phrasings of the same principles, plus forty-eight minor prohibitions. When several new sects came into being during the twelfth and thirteenth centuries, most of the founders were Tendaishū priests who broke away to start their own practices. The precepts these founders had received as Tendaishū priests followed them into the new sects they founded.

For the Zen sects, the emphasis was placed on the practice of zazen. Inasmuch as zazen is a motionless, silent practice, it is impossible to violate the grave prohibitions relating to actions and words. Because zazen is also a practice of concentration, any violations of the grave prohibitions relating to thought must constitute lapses from the state of zazen. So to the extent that one is involved in zazen, violation of precepts is not an issue. It was assumed, as Dōgen explicitly stated, that the practice of zazen automatically leads to a life in accordance with Buddhist principles, as embodied in the precepts.

Until the Meiji Restoration (1868), Buddhism was regulated by the Japanese government, a system inherited from China along with Buddhism itself. Among the government-enforced requirements for clerics were interpretation of the first grave prohibition (not to kill) as banning the eating of meat, a difference in the wording of the third grave prohibition (not to engage in wrongful sexual activity) so that for clerics it was phrased as banning any sexual activity, and a regulation stating that clerics must wear "suitable" clothing at all times, meaning that a Buddhist cleric was visually identifiable by the combination of shaved head and distinctive clothing. In April 1872, these government requirements were revoked. Clerical regulations were returned to the realm of the individual Buddhist sects. It should be noted that even before that time, clerics of the Jōdo Shin sect were exempt from the requirements concerning meat eating and celibacy.

With the end of government regulations enforcing celibacy and forbidding marriage for the Buddhist clergy, the precepts wording was revised so that it became identical for clerics and laypeople.

The arithmetically inclined will have determined that there actually are only 101 questions. So that you won't feel cheated, let me point out that several questions include more than one answer, so there are really more than 108 answers.

In Eastern thought, however, the number 108 is not merely the number between 107 and 109. It is the number used to signify "a whole lot." Use of 108 in that meaning dates back at least to the Upanishads, Indian religious writings that were composed primarily between the eighth and fourth centuries B.C.E. One listing mentioned in medieval south Indian works consists of 108 Upanishads, in fact.

Possibly 108 was selected because it is the product of nine times twelve. Nine was widely viewed in the ancient world as the number of completion because it is three times three, and three is the perfect number. According to the discussion of numbers in Mircea Eliade's *Encyclopedia of Religion*, "Twelve (3 x 4; 5 + 7) is the great cosmic number. From Sumer and ancient China onwards, it is the number of the signs of the zodiac and the basis of the sexagesimal system. In many cultures, day and night were divided into twelve hours, the year into twelve months, and gnostic religions speak of twelve aeons."

Today's Japanese Buddhism features 108 in the number of beads used in dedicating a good action to another person (or simply showing respect to the dead), in the number of times the temple bells are struck on New Year's Eve, and as the number of attachments to which humans are prone. A count of the beads in the strands I have showed me that my priests' beads really have 114 beads: 108 basic beads, plus one where the ends of the cord are joined, plus five clear beads that divide the strand into six groups of 18 beads each. The beads used by laypeople and sometimes worn by priests outside of religious service times most often contain 27 beads (one-fourth of 108), but the range of those in my own collection is from 24 to 28.

ABOUT MYSELF

1. Why did you decide to become a Buddhist priest?

Looking back on how I came to be in Tokyo as a Buddhist priest, it seems there has never been a time when I planned a progression and accomplished it. Everything just arose from the circumstances—a good Buddhist teaching in the interwoven being of all phenomena.

The first step on this path probably was a remark over coffee and donuts, at a shop near my home in a Los Angeles suburb, one October morning in 1956. Several women were chatting after delivering children to a morning play group for those, like my son and daughter, who lacked preschool companions near home. I happened to sigh that I needed a part-time job to pay off medical bills (this being before widespread medical insurance). Another mother said her husband worked right across the street in an electronics company and had told her they were looking for a blueprint clerk. That sounded possible. My father had opened a radio and television repair shop when I started high school, and I had helped out there enough to recognize electronic parts names. Within a week, I was busily making lists of drawings to be blueprinted, "part-time" at forty-eight hours a week.

Less than a month was needed to convince me that I did not want a career in blueprinting. Dropping out of college after my junior year as a

166

music major had not prepared me for anything else, though. I looked around the company at other employees. Engineers and technical writers seemed to have more interesting jobs. Taking up engineering appeared a long, hard course, but the technical writers' job looked more approachable. I asked the writers what the requirements were; they said none, as far as they had ever noticed. (In fact, five of the six had engineering degrees, and the other had a degree in English.) So a campaign started to get me transferred to technical writing. That turned out to be so much fun that I am still doing it from time to time.

This start was great good fortune because the other writers were unusually well experienced and willing to share their knowledge. The volatility of the aerospace industry, however, soon led that company into decline and sent me through a series of short jobs after that. The next steps happened at a rocket motor development company. I had been hired to write instruction manuals and project reports, and was assigned after a while to write a monthly in-house newsletter. When a new manager was hired for writing new business proposals, I was asked to help him. After two days it was clear he had no idea how to start or what to do. The new manager abruptly became the ex-manager, and I became the sole writer-editor on the proposal team, consisting of a half-dozen engineers and a pair of accountants. It was not the way I would choose to learn a new job, but it certainly was challenging. Shortly afterward, the company hired another proposal manager and created a technical publications department, once more giving me more-experienced fellow workers from whom to learn. Meantime, my marriage had ended in divorce and my salary provided the only support for my two children and myself.

In 1961, a colleague from my first job hired me in the publications department of a Lockheed division with contracts ranging from aircraft servicing and maintenance, through making flight data and voice recorders (the two "black boxes" sought after a crash), to checking species diversity changes near the cooling water outlets of nuclear power plants. Most of the technical writers preferred to specialize in one product line, so I was given "everything else," a post that proved a source of fascinating information.

When a time-sharing computer service was installed, I was assigned to learn how to use it, then pass the information along to the rest of my department. (By this time, I was part of the research and development department.) That was my first involvement with computers. I found them more fun than Santa's visits! After the in-house course, I took courses in BASIC programming language and in business systems analysis, both given on Saturdays by a university extension center. Southern California was, and still seems to be, remarkably blessed with opportunities for continuing education in every field.

Having gotten back into the swing of schooling, when work slowed down a little I decided to try finishing up a B.A. The Pomona campus of California State Polytechnic University was conveniently located between my home and workplace, so I enrolled there in the language arts department as a journalism major (the closest thing to technical writing then available). A year later I graduated with a bachelor of science degree—I have never known why language arts was considered an area of science. An English literature professor had asked me to recommend a technical writing textbook for a course required of all engineering students. I looked at many texts, but they all seemed to concentrate on research papers rather than the everyday writing work of young engineers. So for my undergraduate thesis, I wrote a more directly useful text, published two years later by Kendall-Hunt. With incredible bravery, the professor who had asked my advice ended up teaching a course with my material while I was writing it. Most of the time, I was only a week or so ahead of her!

All this led to my being asked to teach the course myself, as a part-time lecturer. Lockheed was cooperative, so I was able to accept. That meant attending graduation ceremonies, and I didn't want to be one of the handful of people in bachelor's robes while almost everyone else wore doctor's hoods. I promptly enrolled in an evening M.B.A. course, designed to attract aerospace personnel.

Partway through the course, I took a year off from study to install a computer system for which I was system designer, and to complete its software, at the All Nippon Airways maintenance facility in Tokyo. The "crash data recorders" that are read only after an accident or incident in the United States are required to be read routinely in Japan. The computer system automated checking of the tapes. The allotted six months stretched to ten months in Tokyo. That gave me time to explore a bit and become slightly acquainted with Japanese customs and culture. Sightseeing in Japan, I found, often centered on Buddhist temples, giving me an interest in a religion I had barely encountered until then. Statues of Kannon Bodhisattva particularly caught my interest. After returning home, I looked in a public library for information on Kannon's role in

Buddhism. I didn't find that information, but I came upon a book called *Zen Mind, Beginner's Mind* by the Reverend Shunryu Suzuki.

Over the next few months I read that book several times. My children had both established their own homes before I went to Japan, and my second marriage had finally collapsed while I was overseas. The practice of zazen recommended by Rev. Suzuki sounded as though it might aid me in getting through a bitter divorce and learning to live alone. The book described its author as a part of Japan's Sōtō sect, so I looked for a Sōtōshū temple in the Los Angeles area. It was the yellow pages of a Los Angeles telephone book that provided an introduction to Zenshuji Soto Mission, only a few blocks from the city hall and even fewer from the city's "Little Tokyo." I called to ask about zazen instruction in English and was told to arrive fifteen minutes early for the zazen service held every Monday evening. That was the beginning.

Not long after graduating with an M.B.A. I accepted an offer to become part of an organization for new business proposals at Lockheed Missiles and Space, in the San Francisco Bay area. Luckily there is a Sōtōshū temple (Sokoji) in San Francisco also, and I was able to participate in its activities. At work, once more I was given the opportunity to learn a little about dozens of rather esoteric subjects. Proposal work, however, is notoriously wearing on the workers, with eighty-hour weeks common near the deadline date. (And if the deadline is missed by even a minute, several million dollars of company funds will have been totally wasted.) Late in 1978, I asked for a year's leave of absence to study Sōtōshū Zen in Japan. This was dictated not by an overwhelming dedication to Zen practice but rather by an overwhelming weariness. I went to discover whether I could live quietly with less-demanding work and a work week nearer twenty hours than eighty.

My earlier ten months in Tokyo let me observe that English-language technical writers and editors were in short supply and great demand. It was easy to obtain freelance work I could do at home, on my own schedule. Before the year of leave time was over, I had a contract to work exclusively for one translation agency and receive a monthly salary. That month-at-a-time contract continued, with a few lapses, for fourteen years. I still do a little freelance work for the same company. My years of learning how to learn paid off when I was faced all alone with a milling and boring machine manual one month and a journal paper on LSI fabrication the next.

Before the leave year was over, I also had established a zazen room in my tiny apartment. The Reverend Zendō Matsunaga, the bilingual priest of a "Zen center" created by a Japanese woman in a former boutique, had to devote full time to his own temple in Shizuoka Prefecture only five months after I had begun participation in the center. His replacement spoke only Japanese, so the founder decided all non-Japanese would have to find another place for their Zen practice. I offered to share my zazen time at home with anyone who wished to join me. Perhaps stunned by the sudden eviction from the center's activities, I did not pause to realize that in doing so I became the de facto leader, teacher, even priest. When that fact finally dawned on me (a Zen awakening?), I decided to seek training for the job.

In this case, there was no handy extension course to take. The way to learning was entry into the Sōtōshū priesthood as a trainee. Rev. Matsunaga, whom I had first met at Zenshuji in Los Angeles, kindly agreed to accept me as an apprentice. After ten years of training as nonstandard as my other efforts had been, I was accredited as a full priest. During that period I had become an assistant at Taisōji, a temple in central Tokyo headed by the Reverend Kōshō Hatamoto, a long-time friend of my master. For many years after my accreditation, I served as the sole assistant priest at Taisōji. Luckily apprentices of Rev. Hatamoto were able to take over my duties at the end of 1995, when I returned to the Los Angeles area as caregiver for my father, whose health was rapidly failing. After his death in November 1996, I arranged to return to Tokyo and Taisōji as soon as I could settle the legal formalities connected with the death.

Here I am, and here I hope to stay until my bones become earth in a temple cemetery.

2. Why did you write this book?

The idea for this book came from a member of Taisōji's zazen group. One of our Sunday evening meetings occurred soon after an American tour group had visited, and in my talk that evening I mentioned a question raised by one tourist. During the conversation time after zazen, someone asked more about the question. He then suggested that I should write a book to make answers to such questions more available.

Despite my initial rejection of the idea, I reflected on the matter for several weeks. Many of the questions posed by tour group members or lecture attendees, and those raised privately by zazen participants, concern matters rarely addressed in Zen talks. Although the questions might arise from simple curiosity, the answers often rest on teachings and history that cannot be quickly explained. The visiting tourists and attendees at outside lectures to nonreligious organizations, I suddenly realized, often receive information that is not readily available even to long-term zazen participants. Part of the reason seemed to be that outsiders were more willing to ask questions, even questions they thought I might reject as trivial or as unnecessarily personal. The fact that even Zen outsiders wished to ask a question, though, indicated to me that the answer held some significance for the questioner. The book concept became more reasonable to me as I came to view it as a means of communication with many people I could not otherwise reach. It also offered the chance to present more complete discussions than are possible in an ordinary question session.

In considering what matters should be included, I tried for the most part to exclude things that are competently discussed in existing books. The matter of "competently discussed" gained new meaning when I observed an extended series of messages on a Zen-related Internet mailing list that concerned the usage of the term rōshi. Views were energetically debated without any of the participants showing an awareness that the term is used quite differently in different Zen sects (and sometimes even in different Western Zen centers that are nominally of the same sect). As a result, I have tried to address some topics that have different answers according to the group in which the topics arise.

Another criterion was the amount of completely false information that I have heard or read, often from Zen priests or scholars who really should know better. Many Western writers seem convinced that women had no role in Buddhism, and particularly in Zen Buddhism, until the past half century. I have heard more than one Japanese Zen priest state confidently that female priests are forbidden to marry although male priests are allowed to, or that female priests are required to have longer formal training than male priests (and that non-Japanese priests are required to have longer training than Japanese priests). A simple reference to their own sect's regulations would have shown these statements to be false; apparently the speakers had never troubled themselves to read the regulations.

Lastly, I tried to select topics about which many people are curious, regardless of their connection or lack of connection with any form of Buddhism. Angels, for example, have been a popular topic in Christian writing over the past decade or so, so I wanted to include some mention of that topic.

In presenting answers to the questions I had collected, I found my own ignorance reflected at many points. This led to inquiries and research that have certainly improved my own understanding. I hope the resulting book will have the same salutary effect on its readers.

Perfection is not a condition of this transient life, so errors doubtless remain despite my best efforts. For those remaining, I apologize.

SOURCE MATERIALS

ZEN IN THEORY

QUESTION 3

Translation of title *Fukanzazengi* from Yusen Kashiwahara and Koyu Sonada, eds., *Shapers of Japanese Buddhism* (Tokyo: Kosei Publishing, 1994); text quoted from Shohaku Okumura, ed. and trans., *Shikantaza: An Introduction to Zazen* (Kyoto: Kyoto Soto Zen Center, 1985), 40–41 and 42.

QUESTION 4

The koan concerning making a mirror appears in Steven Heine, *Dōgen and the Koan Tradition: A Tale of Two* Shōbōgenzō *Texts* (Albany: SUNY Press, 1994), 6.

QUESTION 5

The first two paragraphs are based on Isshu Miura and Ruth Fuller Sasaki, *The Zen Koan* (San Diego: Harcourt Brace, 1993), 23–30. The quotation starting "Proficiency in zazen" appears on page xi of the same work.

QUESTION 6

Definitions are from Koh Masuda, ed., *Kenkyusha's New Japanese-English Dictionary,* 4th ed. (Tokyo: Kenkyūsha, 1974), 1,450.

QUESTION 7
The "floating" incident appears in Philip Kapleau, *The Three Pillars of Zen* (Boston: Beacon Press, 1967). The koan concerning Kyogen is from the *Sanbyakusoku;* heard during dharma talk by the Reverend Zendō Matsunaga.

QUESTION 12
The *Mumonkan* is available in several translations: Zenkei Shibayama, *Zen Comments on the Mumonkan* (New York: New American Library, 1975); Katsuki Sekida, ed., *Two Zen Classics: Mumonkan and Hekiganroku* (New York: Weatherhill, 1977); and Kōun Yamada, *Gateless Gate* (Los Angeles: Center Publications, 1979). I have slightly rephrased case 41, "Daruma Pacifies a Mind," from the Sekida version.

QUESTION 13
The account of Zen sickness and healing appears in Hakuin Zenji, *The Embossed Tea Kettle: Orate Gama and Other Works by Hakuin Zenji* (London: George Allen & Unwin, 1963), 33–47.

QUESTION 18
Shunryu Suzuki, *Zen Mind, Beginner's Mind* (New York: Weatherhill, 1970).

ZAZEN IN PRACTICE

QUESTION 1
Several translations of the *Fukanzazengi* are available. I have used the one contained in Shohaku Okumura, ed. and trans., *Shikantaza: An Introduction to Zazen* (Kyoto: Kyoto Soto Zen Center, 1985), 39–44.

QUESTION 5
For comparison of thoughts to digestive fluids, see Kosho Uchiyama, *The Zen Teaching of "Homeless" Kodo* (Tokyo: Sotoshu Shumucho, 1990), 121.

WHAT IS A ZEN PRIEST?

QUESTION 2
The history of monasticism, the quote starting "According to this etymology," and that starting "Monastic life in contrast," are taken from the section on "Monasticism" in Mircea Eliade, ed., *Encyclopedia of Religion*

(New York: Macmillan Publishing, 1987) vol. 10, 35–36. The quote starting "The priest, first, performs" is from the section on "Priesthood" in the
same work, vol. 11, 528.

QUESTION 4

The answer is closely based on Sōtōshū Shūmuchō, *Sōtōshūhō Shigatsugō
Bessatsu: Sōtōshū Shūsei* (Tokyo: Sōtōshū Shūmuchō, 1995), 271–320.

QUESTION 5

The answer briefly summarizes the regulations in Rinzaishū Myōshinjiha
Shūmuhonjo, *Rinzaishū Myōshinjiha Shūsei* (Kyoto: Rinzaishū Myōshinjiha Shūmuhonjo, 1997).

QUESTION 6

Historical information is based on Richard Mark Jaffe, "Neither Monk
nor Layman: The Debate over Clerical Marriage in Japanese Buddhism,
1868–1937" (Ph.D. diss., Yale University, 1995), 3–16.

QUESTION 9

The schedule in this answer is a slightly modified version of that given in
Martin Roth and John Stevens, *Zen Guide* (New York: Weatherhill, 1985),
75–76.

QUESTION 10

Statistics in the first two paragraphs are from Bunkachō, *Shūkyō Nenkan*
(Tokyo: Gyōsei, 1996), 33, 75.

English translations of the "Raihai-tokuzui" include (among others):
Kosen Nishiyama and John Stevens, trans., "Raihaitokuzui: Making a
prostration and attaining the marrow" in *A Complete English Translation
of Dōgen Zenji's Shōbōgenzō (The Eye and Treasury of the True Law)* vol. 2
(Tokyo: Nakayama Shobō, 1977), 158–62; Yuho Yokoi, "Raihai-tokuzui
(Realizing the Essence [of the Way] by Making a Venerative Bow)" in *The
Shobo-genzo* (Tokyo: Sankibo Buddhist Bookstore, 1986), 349–56. A more
complete Japanese text is given in Ian Kishizawa, *Shōbōgenzō Zenkō*
(Tokyo: Daihōrinkaku, 1972), vol. 3, 169–346.

QUESTION 11

The absence of regulations concerning marriage can be verified in Sōtōshū
Shūmuchō, *Sōtōshūhō Shigatsugō Bessatsu: Sōtōshū Shūsei* (Tokyo: Sōtōshū
Shūmuchō, 1995). This answer is based generally on Richard Mark Jaffe,
"Neither Monk nor Layman: The Debate over Clerical Marriage in

Japanese Buddhism, 1868–1937" (Ph.D. diss., Yale University, 1995), and the quote strarting "from now on" appears on page 8 of that work..

QUESTION 14
Data are from Sōtōshū Shūmuchō, *Sōtōshū Shūsei Sōgō Chōsa Hōkokusho* (Tokyo: Sōtōshū Shūmuchō, 1995); yen-dollar conversions were calculated at 102.3 yen per dollar, the 1994 annual average given in Douglas Ostrum, "Yen's Rally Continued in 1999," in *Japan Economic Institute Review*, No. 3, Jan 21, 2000.

WHAT ARE ZEN RELIGIOUS SERVICES LIKE?

QUESTION 3
The discussion of the meaning of "sutra" is based on Kogen Mizuno, *Buddhist Sutras: Origin, Development, Transmission* (Tokyo: Kosei Publishing, 1982). The sutras used by Sōtōshū are specified in Sōtōshū Shūmuchō, *Sōtōshūchō Shigatsugō Bessatsu: Sōtōshū Shūsei* (Tokyo: Sōtōshū Shūmuchō, 1995), 639–640.

QUESTION 7
The translations of sutra passages and of the general dedication are quoted from Soto Shumucho, *Soto Shu Sutras* (Tokyo: Soto Shumucho 1984), English pages 5, 29, and 30 for sutra passages and 21 for the dedication. My translation of the memorial service dedication is based on Sōtōshū Shūmuchō, *Sōtōshū Nikka Gongyō Seiten* (Tokyo: Sōtōshū Shūmuchō, 1990), 235–37.

QUESTION 9
The last paragraph is based on information from Harald Fuess, "Quick and Slow: Interpreting Declining Divorce Prior to 1940," chapter 6 in *Divorce in Japan* (Palo Alto, CA: Stanfor University Press, forthcoming).

QUESTION 13
The discussion of early translations from Indic languages into Chinese is based on Kogen Mizuno, *Buddhist Sutras: Origin, Development, Transmission* (Tokyo: Kosei Publishing, 1982), 52–55.

QUESTION 14
The story of the origin of Obon is based on Zenno Ishigami, ed., *Disciples of the Buddha* (Tokyo: Kosei Publishing, 1989), 25–26.

QUESTION 17

The Four Seals of the Law and the Twelve-Linked Chain of Dependent
Origination are quoted, with slight modifications, from Kogen Mizuno,
Essentials of Buddhism (Tokyo: Kosei Publishing, 1996), 121, 142–143.

WHAT TITLES AND HONORIFICS ARE
USED FOR ZEN PRIESTS?

QUESTION 5

This answer is based on Robert H. Sharf, "Sanbōkyōdan: Zen and the
Way of the New Religions," *Japanese Journal of Religious Studies* 22 nos.
3–4 (1995): 417–58.

WHAT CHARACTERIZES JAPANESE BUDDHISM
OVERALL AND ZEN BUDDHISM IN PARTICULAR?

QUESTION 3

This exceedingly brief review of the varieties of Japanese Buddhism is
drawn from three books: Bukkyo Dendo Kyokai, *Buddhist Denominations
and Schools in Japan* (Tokyo: Bukkyo Dendo Kyokai, 1984); Bunkachō,
Shukyō Nenkan (Tokyo: Gyōsei, 1996); and Yusen Kashiwahara and Koyu
Sonada eds., *Shapers of Japanese Buddhism* (Tokyo: Kosei Publishing,
1994).

QUESTION 6

The quote starting "for many Japanese" is a citation of a Japanese work in
Ian Reader, *Religion in Contemporary Japan* (London: Macmillan, 1991), 14.

QUESTION 9

The story about Shinran Shōnin is told in Yusen Kashiwahara and Koyu
Sonada eds., *Shapers of Japanese Buddhism* (Tokyo: Kosei Publishing,
1994), 87.

QUESTION 10

The English version of the sixteen precepts is slightly modified from
Kogen Mizuno, *Essentials of Buddhism* (Tokyo: Kosei Publishing, 1996),
170–71.

QUESTION 11

The last two paragraphs are based generally on Richard Mark Jaffe, "Neither Monk nor Layman: The Debate over Clerical Marriage in Japanese Buddhism, 1868–1937" (Ph.D. diss., Yale University, 1995).

QUESTION 12

The significance of 108 is derived from the "Numbers" section of Mircea Eliade, ed., *Encyclopedia of Religion* (New York: Macmillan Publishing, 1987).

GLOSSARY

administrative headquarters of sect = *shūmuchō*
The organization within a sect that deals with administrative matters, as distinguished from religious matters.

bhikkhu, bhikshu
The Pali and Sanskrit terms for a male Buddhist cleric.

bhikkhuni, bhikshuni
The Pali and Sanskrit terms for a female Buddhist cleric.

Bodhidharma
The Indian cleric (470?–528?) said to have transmitted the Zen branch of Buddhism to China.

bowl scraper = *setsu*
A lacquered wooden utensil, similar in size and shape to an ordinary tongue depressor, with a small piece of fabric over one end for cleaning one's set of eating bowls.

Buddha
An Indic term meaning Awakened One. Where capitalized in this book, it means the person we now call Shakyamuni Buddha, who lived

about 2,500 years ago, unless another name (e.g., Amida) is used with Buddha. Without a capital, it refers to any fully awakened being.

buddha robe = *o-kesa, kesa*
The rectangular garment tied at the left shoulder that is worn by Buddhist clerics either as the sole outer garment or as the outermost garment.

Buddhism
A world religion started about 2,500 years ago, based on the teachings of Shakyamuni Buddha.

Chinese-style robe = *koromo*
A garment with wide, long sleeves that is worn by Japanese Buddhist clerics beneath the buddha robe.

clergy
Those persons certified as religious professionals and leaders by an organized religion (gender-neutral term).

cleric
A member of the clergy of an organized religion (gender-neutral term).

Confucianism
A religion based on the teachings of the Chinese philosopher Confucius (551–479 B.C.E.).

dharma
The principles that order the universe; the teachings of Shakyamuni Buddha and his followers.

Dōgen
A Japanese cleric, Dōgen Kigen (1200–1253), who brought the Sōtō teachings to Japan and who founded Eiheiji, one of Sōtōshū's two head temples.

Eightfold Path
A companion teaching to the Four Noble Truths, specifying the path that leads to the cessation of unsatisfactoriness (right views, right

thoughts, right speech, right action, right livelihood, right effort, right
mindfulness, and right concentration).

Eiheiji
One of Sōtōshū's two head temples, founded by Dōgen and located in Fukui Prefecture.

Four Noble Truths
The first teaching of Shakyamuni Buddha (the truth of unsatisfactoriness; the truth of the origin of unsatisfactoriness; the truth of the cessation of unsatisfactoriness; the truth of the path that leads to the cessation of unsatisfactoriness).

head temple = *daihonzan*
The leading temple of a particular sect, under which all temples of the sect were required to be organized until the Meiji Restoration and, in most cases, remain organized even today.

ihai, o-ihai
See memorial plaque.

Jōdo Shinshū
The Japanese Buddhist sect founded by Shinran and its modern offshoots.

Jōdoshū
The Japanese Buddhist sect founded by Hōnen and its modern offshoots.

jūshoku
See resident priest.

just sitting = *shikan taza*
Seated concentration on direct experience of each moment.

kanchō
The chief priest of an organized Buddhist sect.

kanna zen
See koan practice.

kanshū
In Sōtōshū, the chief priest of one of the two head temples; the two kanshū serve alternate terms as kanchō of Sōtōshū.

keisaku
See *kyosaku.*

kenshō
A term for Buddhist awakening or seeing the real nature of oneself and the universe.

kesa
See buddha robe.

kinhin
See walking zazen.

koan
A brief episode encapsulating a particular Buddhist teaching.

koan practice = *kanna zen*
Concentration on an assigned koan.

koromo
See Chinese-style robe.

kyosaku = *keisaku*
A long stick, rounded at one end and flat at the other, used to strike the shoulder muscles of persons doing zazen to relieve their drowsiness or relax the back and shoulder muscles.

laics = laypeople = laypersons
All people who are not clerics.

lineage
In Zen terms, a lineage is a succession from master to apprentices to the apprentices' apprentices, etc., through several "generations."

lotus position
A sitting position; in the full-lotus position *(kekka fuza)*, both feet rest
on the opposite thighs, whereas in the half-lotus position *(hanka fuza)*,
only one foot rests on the opposite thigh while the other foot rests on
the sitting surface.

master
The person to whom someone is apprenticed.

meditation
Contemplation of a topic or text, especially one of a religious nature.

Meiji Restoration
The coup d'etat in 1868 that ended government under a series of
military leaders called shoguns and initiated a government directly
under the hereditary emperor.

memorial marker = *tōba, o-tōba*
An upright slat of unfinished wood that is shaped at the top to represent the five elements of ancient India and, thus, to symbolize a
Buddhist temple; the occasion for making the symbolic offering of a
temple, the precepts name of the person in whose memory it is offered,
and the name of the donor are written on the front using brush and ink.

memorial plaque = *ihai, o-ihai*
An upright wooden plaque, usually lacquered and having engraved characters, showing the precepts name and death date of a deceased person on
the front and that person's civil name and age at death on the back.

miniature buddha robe = *rakusu*
A small version of the buddha robe, with a strap for suspending it
around the neck and in front of the chest.

monasticism
The formal institution underlying the life of monastics.

monastics
Clerics or laics living communally in seclusion from society; strictly
speaking, the term monastics applies only to those who maintain permanent separation from ordinary life, devoting themselves solely to

their own religious practice and having no contact with anyone outside the walls of the monastery in which they live.

monk
A male monastic.

nembutsu
Repeated invocation of a particular buddha, especially Amida Buddha.

nun
A female monastic.

Ōbakushū
A Japanese Buddhist sect based on Rinzai teachings, with a total of 464 temples reported in 1995.

o-toba
See memorial marker.

precepts
The guiding principles by which Buddhists seek to live.

precepts ceremony
The rite of receiving the Buddhist precepts from a priest, either to enter the priesthood as that priest's apprentice *(shukke tokudo)* or to formally become a Buddhist layperson *(zaike tokudo)*.

precepts name
A name bestowed by the priest who gives the precepts to someone.

priest
A cleric; various religions use other terms for their clerics, but this is the English term traditionally used for the clerics of Japanese Buddhism and is used by many other religions (gender-neutral term).

priests hall = *sōdō*
The building in which priests, especially priest-trainees, do zazen, eat, and sleep during sesshin and training periods.

rakusu
> See miniature buddha robe.

resident priest = *jūshoku*
> The main (usually sole) priest of a temple, who is responsible for the temple and its functions.

Rinzai
> The founder of one branch of Zen Buddhism, a Chinese cleric named Lin-chi I-hsuan (?–867), called Rinzai Gigen in Japanese; also the Zen branch founded by Rinzai Gigen, and the teachings of that branch, characterized by koan practice.

Rinzaishū
> The Japanese Zen Buddhist sects based on Rinzai teachings, now consisting of fifteen independent sects with a total of 5,742 temples reported in 1995.

satori
> The experience of Buddhist awakening.

seiza
> Literally, correct sitting; the posture conventionally used (especially on formal occasions) for sitting on tatami, with buttocks resting on heels and back erect in a straight line.

sesshin
> A period of intensive practice of zazen, of either the just sitting or the koan practice type, during which participants do essentially nothing except zazen; the duration is typically three to seven days.

shikan taza
> See just sitting.

Shinto
> The Way of the Kami, an indigenous Japanese religion based on *kami* (spirits of persons or natural objects).

Shugendō
> A Japanese religion based on mountain asceticism, having elements of esoteric Buddhism as well.

shukke tokudo
See precepts ceremony.

shūmuchō
See administrative headquarters.

sōdō
See priests hall.

Sōjiji
One of Sōtōshū's two head temples, founded by Keizan Jōkin (1268–1325) and now located in Yokohama, Kanagawa Prefecture.

Sōtō
A branch of Zen Buddhism based on the teachings of Chinese clerics Tung-shan Liang-chieh (807–69), called Tōzan Ryōkai in Japanese, and Ts'ao-shan Pen-chi (840–901), called Sōzan Honjaku in Japanese; also the teachings of that branch, characterized by just sitting *(shikan taza)*.

Sōtōshū
The Japanese sect based on the Sōtō teachings, which is a single sect with 14,702 temples reported in 1995.

sutra
A Buddhist religious text recognized as conveying the direct teachings of Shakyamuni Buddha; this term is often used in the much broader meaning of any Buddhist religious text.

takuhatsu
The Buddhist religious practice of accepting donations of food or money while chanting sutras, especially as performed in a group while walking.

Tendaishū
The Japanese Buddhist sect founded by Saichō and its modern off-shoots.

Twelve-Linked Chain of Dependent Origination
The Buddhist teaching showing how all phenomena are both causes and effects of other phenomena.

walking zazen = *kinhin*

Walking performed between intervals of zazen.

zabuton

A thin, square cushion used for sitting on tatami and for zazen.

zafu

A thick, round cushion used for zazen.

zaike tokudo

See precepts ceremony.

zazen

Seated concentration.

Zen

The branch of Japanese Buddhism that emphasizes concentration.

The "weathermark" identifies this book as a production of Weatherhill, Inc., publishers of fine books on Asia and the Pacific. Book and cover design: D.S. Noble. Production supervision: Bill Rose. Printing and Binding: R.R. Donnelly. The typeface used is Adobe Garamond, with Scala Sans and Quadraat for display.